Line of Lost Lives

Line of Lost Lives

by

J. S. Cosford

GRYPHON
BOOKS

First published 1988
First reprinted 1989

Copyright © J. S. Cosford 1988

ISBN: 0 9513666 0 2

Printed and bound by Woolnough Bookbinding, Irthlingborough, Northants.

Contents

Acknowledgements
Foreword
Dedication
Introduction
1 Roll Call 1
2 Preparations 6
3 Fierce Fighting Begins 10
4 Burnt 16
5 Singapore Capitulates 20
6 River Valley 33
7 Changi 42
8 Selarang 45
9 Train to Thailand 55
10 Chungkai 63
11 Christmas 1942 and Dysentery 70
12 Bridge Building 76
13 Nom Pradai and Wun Lun 82
14 Trains and Pigs 88
15 Tamarkan 93
16 Medical Orderly 98
17 Back to Chungkai 106
18 A Policeman in Chungkai 115
19 Takunun and Bombing 124
20 Another Christmas 135
21 Chungkai Again 139
22 Beasts of Burden 143
23 Wampo 150
24 "Nobby, Horse Doctor" 155
25 Tamuang 164
26 No Good House 169
27 Good News 175
28 Freedom 182
29 On the Move 190
30 Summing Up 196

Acknowledgements

My thanks are due to daughter Sue for typing and retyping what must have seemed endless pages of near illegible hand writing. To son-in-law Malcolm for his assistance with the photocopying. To daughter Dee for her interpretation of ideas into presentable artwork, the sketches and cover design. To daughter Elizabeth for her constructive criticism and to son Mike for his skill with the camera.

Finally to my wife, Elizabeth, for the encouragement, understanding and patience she displayed over the long period during which 'Line of Lost Lives' was being written, and when our home, at times, resembled that of an untidy waste paper collection point.

List of Illustrations

New Testament 28
Pages inside New Testament 29
POW Number and Identity Discs 34
Selerang Incident 48
Photograph of Exterior of Wagon 56
POW's in Railway Wagon 57
'Pom Pom' Boat 61
Making Railway Embankment 65
Map of Area 1 74
Map of Area 2 75
Bridge Building 78
Thai Woman 87
Chungkai Cutting 94
Burning Cholera Victims 97
Ulcer Ward 99
Operation in Jungle 100
Page from Army Pay Book 103
Large Camp 107
Wampo Bridge 126
Beasts of Burden 147
Tamarkan Bridges 159
'No Good House' 171
Leaflet 183
Pamphlet regarding Malaria 193
Photograph of Medical Card 194
Hints on Diet 195
Doug Skippen in Kanchanaburi Cemetery 199
Plaque 199
Roll of Honour 200

Photograph of Tamarkan Bridge.................................... 201
Photograph of Diesel Lorry 201
Photograph of Letters regarding Pension........................... 202
Photograph of Author, 1987, after Medals stolen.................. 202

The drawings by the late Charles Thrale, another member of the Cambridgeshire Regiment, are reproduced by courtesy of his daughter, Mrs Doreen Collins and the Imperial War Museum.

Foreword

John Cosford went into battle as a junior non commissioned officer in the 1st Battalion The Cambridgeshire Regiment, part of the newly arrived 18th East Anglian Division, during the last days of The Malayan Campaign and The Siege of Singapore.

This is his story of the fighting for, and the fall of Singapore, and of the following long and arduous years as a Prisoner of War of the Japanese. He does not concern himself with strategy, or the rights and wrongs of the decisions by commanders and politicians. He concentrates on the problem of the day to day struggle to survive in the very harshest of circumstances.

It is a story of heroism by many, and of despicable actions by a very few. It tells of almost unimaginable hardships and of brutal treatment, of living in squalor and degradation, of suffering, disease and death. But above all it tells a story of how The British Soldier, through self discipline, and pride in himself, his comrades, his Regiment and his Country, managed to survive.

I was fascinated to read this very vivid story. As Colonel of The Royal Anglian Regiment, of which The Cambridgeshire Regiment is now part, I am privileged to write this foreword. I salute John Cosford, and all his comrades, who by their staunch and resolute behaviour, maintained, whatever the costs to themselves, the standards which have made the British Army what it is, and what it always will be as long as men, such as they, continue to serve.

General Sir Timothy Creasey, KCB, OBE

Post Script
Sadly General Sir Timothy Creasey did not live to see the book published. His widow, Lady Annette Creasey, has kindly agreed that the foreword should be used as Sir Timothy had said he felt privileged to be associated with the work.

Dedication

To all who fought in the defence of Singapore and eventually became Prisoners of War in Japanese hands, especially the men of the Cambridgeshire Regiment.

Also to the memory of the unfortunate thousands who failed to return home.

Introduction

Line of Lost Lives is not fiction. It is an account of my personal experience as a Prisoner of War in Japanese hands during the period February 1942 to September 1945.

Much of the narrative deals with life in various camps in Thailand, and the conditions experienced whilst working on the now infamous railway, built from Thailand to Burma. It has been written without any attempt at exaggeration, sensationalism or glorification. It is a true account of what was taking place during those unforgettable years. Some names have been invented but the narration of all incidents where I was personally involved are authentic. The few stories concerning other men or locations are, to the best of my knowledge true, or typical of events at that time.

The first chapters record my experience of the fighting preceding the capitulation of Singapore. I consider this section of the book to be extremely important. Even now, after the lapse of some forty odd years, I find people who still have the mistaken conviction that the Island was handed over without a fight, and that British soldiers became prisoners without putting up any resistance, or firing a 'shot in anger'.

This ill-informed misconception must be corrected and the record put straight.

Perhaps there were troops who found themselves in that unsatisfactory situation, but it would not have been of their own volition. However, this, most definitely, was not the experience of the Cambridgeshire Regiment or, no doubt, many other front line troops. Our battalion fought fiercely, without conceding any ground, became surrounded by the enemy and still continued to resist strongly after the cease fire was supposed to have taken effect.

Many brave men were killed in the action, countless others being wounded and dying within a few days or weeks of becoming prisoners.

I am proud to have been one of the "Fen Tigers", a member of the Cambridgeshire Regiment.

Chapter 1

Roll Call

"Is not today enough? Why do I peer into the darkness of the day to come? Is not tomorrow e'er as yesterday?"
Shelley

"Phew! What could I do with a swig of water?" That readily answered question must have been in the forefront of most of our minds, and I suspect no doubt closely followed by another. "What would I like to do with that pig of a Sergeant Major: given half the chance?"

A couple of hundred men of an Infantry Regiment, average age about twenty, marching in sweltering heat on a dusty plain in India. What had the friendly sadist of a Sergeant Major told us?

"You're all too soft. We're taking you on a little march to toughen you up," he bawled, with a nasty little glint in his eye. "You've had a couple of months luxury cruise from England, now it's back to work. You should all have full water bottles and they had better stay that way until I give the order. Any man caught taking a drink before I say the word will be put on a charge."

How we hated the blighter as he strutted along, carrying only his revolver and water bottle, nothing compared to us, loaded up like donkeys with equipment and rifles. Water! What a precious commodity it is. All of us were to discover in the years that followed how important it is to life, and, that without it many would cease to live.

It was as simple as that. Yes, the self discipline forced upon us by that sergeant major was to stand us in good stead before very long.

As I marched along in tropical kit, and the ugly shorts with the buttoned-up bottoms designed to let down and protect the knees, my thoughts wandered back to the early days of 1939. Had I been unwise in joining the Territorials? Perhaps not, at least I was still with a few friends from civilian life. It seemed years since that measured voice on the radio announced that all Territorials must report at once to their units. Was he actually referring to me? I remembered how I scrambled into my uniform, first donned shyly about six months previously. I had raced up to the office on my bike to tell the Postmaster I had been called up and wouldn't be coming to work.

He had always appeared to be an impatient and grumpy old man, but not on this occasion. I remembered how surprised I was to find normal gruffness replaced by kindliness I'd never even suspected he could muster. Tears in his eyes too. He must have known something that I didn't comprehend. The rest of the staff wished me luck. Their "We'll see you all right" promised future parcels of food and cigarettes. Everything seemed fine. Food and cigarettes, I had no idea what those words would come to mean later. But everything was fine at first, and even later on, after the war with Germany had been going on for some time, when we had been billeted in a camp that had been prepared for German internees, everything was still fine. All the barbed wire we had to clear away before we could adapt the camp for our own purposes, never suggested the prison camps I was to enter on very different terms. Barbed wire casts no shadow!

Apart from extensive training in fitness and fighting, we seemed to have spent the first two years of the war perfecting the art of packing equipment and stores and moving to other locations. Speculation, rumour and constant movement become part of a soldier's life. In the war time army you get used to living a day at a time, and it's only now and again that a break in the routine of seemingly pointless change, gives you the chance of piecing together what's been happening to you.

I think during the first year we must have covered most of Norfolk. Such places as Kimberley Hall, Wymondham, North Walsham, Sea Palling and Stalham. At Stalham I had been fortunate to survive unscathed, when bombs from a German plane had demolished a building in which I was taking a hurried meal. I couldn't understand how, when emerging from all that brick rubble, dust and debris, my legs had managed to become entangled in telephone wires. I didn't even get a new uniform out of the deal! We had been billeted in a tweed mill at Galashiels in Scotland and spent time under canvas in Warwickshire. One can have enough of moving around playing at soldiers and I think when the rumour that we were going abroad for real this time began to gain substance, most of us became somewhat excited and relieved.

Perhaps this was it! We had been issued with tropical kit so that when we were transported to Liverpool in October 1941 it became clear to everybody, except the humourists of the Battalion, that we wouldn't be going to Iceland. We sailed from a fog-bound Liverpool aboard the SS Orcades, not having any idea of our ultimate destination. Our ship was one of a convoy of six and we had an escort of three destroyers as we headed out into the Atlantic.

About halfway across, midst a much exaggerated display of pageantry, our little escort was relieved by the United States Navy. At this time America had not entered the war and we were more than a little surprised to see that an aircraft carrier, two cruisers and about nine destroyers had arrived to accompany our convoy.

At Halifax, Nova Scotia, we transferred to the "West Point", formerly the "America", a much larger ship this time but how they packed us on board like sardines. A long voyage took us to Trinidad and South Africa where we had been allowed a few days shore leave. Like most visitors to Cape Town I visited the Table Mountain, ascending by cable railway. The view from the top should have been spectacular, but like Liverpool it was shrouded in cloud or fog. I wondered if that was to be the pattern of the future. Perhaps it was just as well, foreknowledge of what was to come may well have proved fatal to many of us.

Christmas was spent at sea and soon after we docked at Bombay. One day ashore here was enough for most of us, our eyes were certainly opened as we took in the varying degrees of squalor and privation.

And so on to Ahmednager and the few weeks toughening up process, and how to control one's urge for a drink. I'll always remember the Kite Hawks at that place. We would collect our meal from the cookhouse and carry it some fifty yards, over an open square, to a suitable place to eat. Unless we took great care to protect it, the best part would be lost before we got there. These birds, with their large wings, would swoop down, snatch the food in their claws, and soar away again before the startled man could protest. We called them "Shite Hawks" and used the same term later on to describe some of our own comrades whose conduct left a lot to be desired.

Our spell at Ahmednager over, it was back to Bombay where we boarded the same ship that had taken us there. Within a few hours it was back on the open sea and the thought on most of our minds

"Where to now?". Our short spell in India had taught us, among other things, just how much can be done on a pint of water if only you know the way. Perhaps we were being sent to the African desert, but surely we wouldn't have gone to India first? Still, it's possible we thought, after all we had been nearly all round the world to get here.

Six days out of Bombay we heard the news, we were bound for Singapore, and maps of Malaya were put before us. I remember that the large wall map had little red flags showing the places where the Japs had already landed and a mighty lot of red flags there were. General opinion was that it was only a matter of time before all Malaya and Singapore would be in their hands. I remember how dismayed I was, two days before we landed, to find all the red flags removed. We guessed the position was hopeless but were told that we were to land at all costs, even if it meant sacrificing the ship. We were going to push the Japs back to Japan!

Right back to Japan! Like hell we were, those of us that were left.

But there were still a few at large! They bombed us and we broke convoy. Our ship being the fastest reached Singapore first, engines racing so hard that she vibrated from stem to stern.

Kepel Harbour, Singapore, with twenty seven Japanese bombers concentrating on the docks, but we got in all right without casualties and the smartest piece of military organisation got us from ships to suburbs in record time.

No city has ever turned out to be what I expected and Singapore was certainly no exception. We had always been led to believe that Singapore was a fortress. How wrong that impression had been. Singapore most definitely was not a fortress! From what I could see of it, in our hasty dash to the suburb of Katong, it could have been like any place in Britain except that there appeared to be no precautions for air raids and no military preparations whatsoever.

The houses we were to occupy had Orders of Evacuation in English plastered on the walls, thus strengthening the impression of home. But the coconut palms and banana trees in the garden brought us back to reality and after we had stripped them of their fruit, ignoring the "Don't touch anything" order, we had time to consider the situation.

Everybody had cheered us on our way from the docks, Chinese, Indians, Malays, Tamils and no doubt Japanese too I expect, as the Country was riddled with fifth columnists, but one often-repeated remark about summed the matter up for us, "We don't want troops, we want aircraft." They were soon to say the same thing in England. It's wonderful how news travels!

A hectic two days, getting ready for what? We knew the enemy couldn't be far away. Not much further than the occupants of these houses whose food was still in the "fridge".

Continuous bombing by formations of Japanese planes, twenty seven in each, helped us realise we were in the front line at last. Twenty seven planes dropping their bomb loads simultaneously is pretty shattering, and there were ever increasing numbers of flattened areas to bear witness to their destructive power. "We don't want troops, we want aircraft". Oh hell!

We were also treated to leaflet raids. The civilian population were being advised to vacate the island, and the troops told to lay down their arms as we were beaten, and would never return to our wives and families. I remember one implied that if we surrendered we would be treated like soldiers, it went on, "Resist and you will be given the sword". Another picturing a young mother with children looking at her, posed the question, "When is my daddy coming home?" Yet a third showing a glamorous, curvacious young lady, scantily clothed was captioned, "Oh Tommy, I am so lonely without you!" These planes had complete freedom of the air, never once did I see a British plane do anything to intercept them. There weren't any!

During the two days in which we were getting organised I made several trips to bring back vehicles for our Battalion's use, on these journeys we were constantly bombed but the plight of the refugees crowding the roads was something that had to be seen to be believed. There were thousands of them. It seemed impossible that so much junk, pigs, chickens, ducks, charcoal stoves, and sleeping mats could be loaded on to so few lorries, barrows, trucks and bicycles. Little children not able to walk were slung on their mothers' backs. Everyone looked pitifully tired and apprehensive of the enemy from the rear or the aircraft from above. Everything was in such confusion that it was impossible to tell who were genuine refugees and who were the natives looking forward with pleasure to our defeat, or indeed how many Japs there were among them, they all looked the same to us.

The more wealthy of the civilian population crowded on to the docks, hoping to leave the island before the Japanese arrived. They gave us their cars, keys to houses, anything they couldn't carry, such was their hurry to leave. It made us both angry and disappointed to see RAF personnel board the ship from which we had disembarked.

We were being left to our fate!

Chapter 2

Preparations

"Press we to the field ungrieving. In our heart of hearts believing Victory crowns the just."

Thomas Hardy

Thousands of words have been written and probably will be written as to why Singapore fell. There have been, and no doubt will be many more, versions and accounts of the fighting that took place. There have been, and I suspect, will be even now, forty odd years after the event, various appraisals, inquests, accusations, recriminations from all manner of sources. Opinions of "Top Brass", high ranking Civil Servants, Politicians, Historians and "Armchair Authorities". All of this in retrospect. There have been and no doubt will be reasons put forward of an economic nature. Communists may even be blamed alongside Capitalists.

I do not profess to be able to give an expert opinion on any circumstances leading up to the Capitulation. The account that follows is that of a very junior NCO from an Infantry Battalion. It is limited to my own experiences during those few weeks up to the unconditional surrender.

However, I do know that Singapore, an island approximately thirty five miles long by fifteen miles wide, was definitely not a fortress. When we arrived we saw no evidence to support that description. There were, although I didn't see them, five fifteen inch naval guns pointing out to sea, it was not possible to turn these round to fire at the Japanese advance. I saw no defences, military or civil and certainly no aircraft. I believe there had been obsolete Brewster Buffalows but these had all been destroyed or left the island.

We had no tanks and I saw no sign of anti-tank defences.

After two days of organising during which time we were able to assess, to some extent, the nature of the island we had come to defend, we moved up to the northern coast of Singapore by night. Here my battalion took up positions along an area overlooking the mainland of Malaya. The day we arrived had seen the last of the British Forces withdraw from the mainland and the Causeway blown up.

So this was it.

We were to defend the "Fortress" of Singapore to the last man!

I read somewhere later that Churchill's message to General Wavell was that there must be no surrender. He wanted it made absolutely clear that he expected every inch of ground to be defended, every scrap of material or defences to be blown to pieces to prevent capture by the enemy. There must be protracted fighting among the ruins of Singapore . . .

General Wavell then delivered his instructions to Lt General Percival, the GOC Malayan Forces: "There must be no thought of sparing the troops or the civilian population". We were to fight to the bitter end. No question or thought of surrender was the message to be conveyed to the troops!

Then after a dinner, no doubt in congenial surroundings, he got well out of it and cleared off to Java.

Churchill's and Wavell's idea of a fortress were very different to ours.

The strip of coast which we were to defend, stretching from a deserted Seletar aerodrome to Dixie Village had no defence of any sort until we arrived, but in a few days, working day and night, danert wire, trenches, gun and mortar pits were everywhere. Although under frequent bombing and shelling, and having a number of men wounded, we received no fatal casualties in the first week. We soon discovered that the gun trained on the particular section where I was working usually fired in groups of four. As soon as we heard four muffled reports we knew we had a couple of seconds to get our heads down. Then bang, bang, bang, bang, and we would carry on until it fired again.

The terrain in the area occupied by our battalion was mostly rubber plantation but there were patches of thick jungle and a small area of swamp. The climate was hot and sticky, we were fortunate in not having any rain these first few days, but the mosquitoes were a nuisance. We had been issued with anti-mosquito cream, it smelled horrible and appeared to encourage, rather than deter, the blighters.

There were several days of this sort of action, the occasional bombing, and shells passing over our heads in both directions. Mosquitoes up to now were the chief menace, but it was on the evening of the 8 February 1942 when things 'warmed up' considerably. Our guns started a terrific barrage; thousands of shells passed over us towards the coast on the left of our position. It continued all night and those men resting found it impossible to get a wink of sleep. Everybody was on their toes; the slightest rustle in the jungle was a Jap sneaking round our perimeter camp! We'd all heard of their habit of filtering through the lines and attacking from the rear. The jungle seemed full of moving lights, which of course, were fire flies but as far as we were concerned could have all been Japs. It never occurred to us at the time that had they been the enemy they would hardly carry torches to advertise their presence – surely they would have been as subtle as Gideon's three hundred and put their torches in pitchers.

It was a sleepless night for everybody and in the morning the news of a landing some distance to our left explained the bombardment. The defences had been breached and the Japs were pouring onto the island by the thousand. The barrage continued for most of the day and that evening, my platoon, or the remainder of it, received orders to move into the jungle just behind Seletar Aerodrome on the coast. We moved off at dusk, arriving just after dark and stayed under cover waiting for orders.

History books often describe battles in simple detail, sometimes using diagrams to illustrate the position of opposing forces at various stages of the campaign. British forces in neat little coloured rectangles and wavy lines or different coloured boxes to show the position of the enemy. It is all made to look so simple and uncomplicated, so tidy and orderly. No confusion. Like pushing around pawns on a chess board, or little coloured flags on a map.

But things aren't so neat and well arranged as that in reality. At least not to the soldier who does the fighting. It has occurred to me since I took part in a battle that there were probably English soldiers at Agincourt as bewildered as we were at Singapore. I can imagine one of them saying, "I don't know what we're shooting these bloody arrows at, I haven't seen a perishing Frenchman all day."

Or maybe they arranged things better!

Six of us, two remaining on guard while the others tried to sleep. Four 15 cwt trucks. Shells flying overhead in both directions. Which were ours and which were the enemy's? We didn't know where we were or where the rest of our lot were either. We'd arrived in pitch darkness and been told to wait. We waited. For a shell or the sound of a foreign tongue in the jungle.

At three in the morning my platoon officer ordered me and another driver, Private Twinn, later burnt to death, to follow Captain Spooner, a mortar officer. We followed, it proved extremely difficult, it was very dark, a rough track and, of course, we couldn't use lights. At last we arrived at some underground buildings and our trucks were loaded with mortars and bombs.

Daylight revealed that we were in the bomb dump of Seletar Aerodrome. Orders were that from now on we would come under direct command of Captain Spooner and not our Motor Transport Officer. I was detailed to Sergeant Holihead's detachment, he and two other men of our party of seven were subsequently killed in action. In the early hours of the morning we moved to a position on the airfield that was relatively "warm" as far as shelling was concerned, and remained there for several hours.

About 10.00 hours all platoons and detachments received a message from the Adjutant:

"A small number of Japs have landed on the island. We are going to drive them off. It will be very good experience for us. Like a little scheme in England except that we will be using live ammunition instead of blanks. We shall clear them out in a couple of days. There will be no retreating."

It all sounded very exciting and most of the lads looked forward to the prospect of some real fighting at last. We had been waiting two years for this, now our chance had come.

Chapter 3

Fierce Fighting Begins

> *"Military glory – the attractive rainbow that rises in showers of blood."*
>
> Abraham Lincoln
> 1809-1865

At ten thirty in the morning we moved off towards Singapore. After travelling several miles inland we made northwest heading for Bukit Tima. Progress was slow and the vehicles had to frequently be put under cover to escape the vigilance of enemy aircraft bombing and machine gunning the roads. The Jap planes had complete freedom of the air, the only opposition seemed to come from the small arms fire of the troops on the ground.

The rattle of Bren guns and other small arms fire could be heard in the distance and we could see their planes unchallenged, dive bombing our forward troops. The number of natives going in the opposite direction to us was amazing. Many ambulances and truck loads of wounded men passed us on the way to hospital.

It was getting dusk and the situation fairly quiet when our battalion moved into an area round a small native village. My mortar detachment found themselves shelter in a ramshackle Chinese house and mounted their three inch mortar in the garden. Men were detailed to keep watch and a meal was procured from HQ Company cooks who were making the best of things nearby.

There was little sleep that night. No chance to take your boots off here. Then in the morning after a hurried meal straight from a tin, we set off to meet the enemy. While the rest trudged through jungle and rubber plantations we were to take the trucks up by road the best we could. Mortars, bombs, equipment and a man to assist the driver where necessary. We moved slowly at intervals of about one hundred and seventy five yards, a despatch rider leading the way.

What a journey. Planes swooping low, machine gunning and bombing the whole time. Miraculously, for several hours not a vehicle or man was hit. Then we came to a place under heavy shell fire and were told to make a dash for it, one at a time, pass to some trees further on, get the trucks under cover and await further orders. The Japs must have been able to see every move we made. Their planes were overhead all the time and as we found out later, in radio contact with their troops on the ground.

Our turn came. We both crouched low in the truck. I gave it all the acceleration it would take, in spite of the bursting shells we were through and pulled under cover unscathed. No sooner had we stopped than mortar shells started bursting among us and we received our first casualty. We took cover in an anti-malarial drain, a concrete affair about three feet deep, six inches wide at the bottom and about three feet wide at the top. It was most uncomfortable but it saved our lives. For over an hour this area was plastered with mortar shells but very little damage was done. Sixty per cent seemed to be duds and the rest fell in the right places for us. Two trucks received damage, but could still be driven. That's more than could be said about one of the lad's mess tins. I well remember him standing in the road, completely unperturbed as machine gun bullets kicked up dust all round his feet, holding up the damaged object he was indignantly shouting, "Look what they've done to my bloody mess tin". A piece of shrapnel or bullet had torn a big hole in its centre. At least it wasn't his head!

I saw several other acts of men showing complete disregard for their personal safety, in the face of heavy fire and extreme danger. I couldn't decide if in some cases they were acts of supreme bravery or a complete lack of imagination.

After about two hours, runners came to each of our trucks and told us that our companies were in position, they would take us to our respective detachments. I was to go to Sergeant Holihead, our mortar would be firing with a platoon of 'D' Company.

Despite the attention of enemy planes and some slight shelling we found our positions easily. Our platoon occupied an area just off Adam Road, a residential district, not too far from Bukit Tima. Here were quite large houses with verandahs in front, thirty to forty yards apart and a private road running through the middle of them. They were built on the side of a hill, the backs of the houses being at ground level and the front on concrete or stone pillars several feet high, allowing movement underneath. We had positions around and under these houses, our mortar being mounted on the lawn of the most forward. We appeared to be more or less centre of a line, other companies from our battalion occupying positions on either side.

At four thirty in the afternoon there was no fighting to be heard anywhere in our area. Just an occasional gun and a few planes at intervals. The mortar men and I scrounged some tinned food from the deserted house and the officer commanding the platoon joined us in a scrappy meal of cold stew and pineapple chunks.

No, he didn't know exactly where the Japs were, but he'd sent a corporal and six men to find out. We were to wait in this position and give 'em hell when they arrived. Somewhere to our right were the Suffolks and in front of us the enemy, at any rate, one thing was for certain, there were no troops between us and the Japs.

The war seemed to have ebbed away from us. It didn't seem possible we were going to do any fighting. Surely this was just another exercise! More practice with blanks!

It wasn't!

Suddenly, there was a lot of light machine gun fire to our front. Very shortly after, the corporal and his men returned. Hundreds of Japs were advancing along the road towards us. They were less than three hundred yards away. "They saw us and opened fire, we made ourselves scarce as quickly as possible."

The war had caught up with us again. The information was sent back to Battalion Head Quarters. The OC inspected the defences and issued orders to the NCO's. It was getting dusk and everyone "stood to" for a couple of hours. But the attack didn't come. Some men were allowed to rest while others kept a look out. From this time onward there was precious little sleep for anybody, perhaps the odd snatched nap fully clothed and equipped, no chance of a wash either. God! How we must have stunk!

Just before day break, after a night of unexpected quiet, a terrific din started to our front right. The Japs were attacking 'A' Company. Everyone strained their eyes in the half light. Waiting – just itching to have a bang at these little yellow men. The stories we had heard about them! They were bad shots as they couldn't shut one eye at a time but had to fire with both eyes open! They were wearing PT vests and shorts!

Were they hell!

As it became lighter wounded men took the short cut across our position to the Regimental Aid Post (RAP). They spoke of heavy fighting and many casualties, killed and wounded. Our uniform was khaki drill shorts and shirts, many of the men struggling to reach the RAP looked as though they were wearing red football jerseys, their shirts being saturated with blood. Many had hastily applied field dressings, some with such terrible wounds it was amazing they could walk or crawl the distance. The stretcher bearers were having a busy time and they didn't have enough men or stretchers to cope with the casualties.

It was soon to be our turn. Sgt. Holihead ranged his mortar on the enemy and gave the order to fire. In a second we were all flat on our backs, deafened and blinded, faces stung by embedded grit, steel helmets on the back of our heads. The bomb had struck a twig several feet over our heads and exploded in mid air. It was a miracle we weren't all killed, but no one was hurt. The detachment ranged again and the mortar was soon flinging loads of bombs at the enemy.

Shortly after daylight the air became alive with hot bullets, but we couldn't see the Japs and could only fire where we thought they were. Many received wounds and within a few minutes the platoon sergeant had been killed.

Things were hotting up with a vengeance. From this period until the last day of the fighting I lost all sense of time, dates, and it became difficult to remember in what particular order any events took place. This was the beginning of five days and nights without sleep, rest or a wash. We received nothing to eat or drink from our 'B' Echelon who maintained that we became cut off and it was impossible to get rations to us. We managed to get our water bottles filled once a day and existed on this.

On this first day of the real fighting, as far as we were concerned, most of the firing seemed to be coming from undergrowth and coconut palms about two hundred yards away to our front right. Our houses being built on the side of a hill, below us was a valley on the other side of which was another hill, and it was here the bulk of the enemy appeared to be. It was decided to attack as our mortar and small arms didn't seem to be having much effect. A number of men were sent in while we gave them covering fire, but it was useless and they had to return. Many were wounded. Some were killed and the badly wounded were only brought in with great difficulty and taken to the Regimental Aid Post.

All this day and night the fighting continued. We still couldn't see the Japs. I don't know if they could see us or not but we still received casualties. Perhaps it was the same for them, we could hear their shouting to each other and I'm certain they must have lost a lot of men. An opinion that some of them were firing from the tops of coconut palms led us to fire at likely sniper positions but this produced no obvious results. We did discover later that some Japs had been killed in these positions but they were being held up by straps which prevented their bodies falling.

Meanwhile one of our companies received information that a number of Japs were beside a reservoir. A platoon went through the jungle in single file, holding on to each other's bayonet scabbards as it was dark. They were led by an officer of the FMSUF (Federated Malay State Volunteer Forces) who knew the area well. On reaching the hill overlooking the reservoir, they saw several hundred of their troops on the far side, some even swimming and bathing. Bren guns and two inch mortars were mounted, the remainder of the platoon having rifles. On the order "fire" they were able to account for the greater number of them and return to the battalion in safety although at times passing very close to enemy positions where they could even hear them talking.

Our troubles began to increase. Under cover of darkness a number of Japs managed to take possession of the house next to ours, possibly up to twenty of them in the house itself and others nearby. As it became daylight they gave us a very uncomfortable time, small arms fire was intensive and we occasionally caught sight of a Jap. Try as we might we couldn't completely dislodge them. Many attempts were made to do so but all in vain. As fast as one lot was driven out or killed they were replaced by others during the night. It would have only been a hindrance for us to occupy the building ourselves so we settled down to the idea of having Japs for neighbours, and picked them off one at a time whenever we had the chance.

By this time men from 'C' Company and others had reinforced our depleted numbers. Three attacks were made on the hill opposite but they weren't very successful. Casualties increased in numbers, officers and men killed and wounded. I saw one man have a bullet pass clean through his steel helmet, in the front and out the back, leaving a terrific hole, but the wearer himself was unhurt. Private Newbury, a stretcher bearer pal of mine, was not so fortunate. He was attending a fellow who lived near me in 'Civvy Street', this man was lying on a stretcher with a bad wound to his head, when a bullet from our "next door neighbours" went in the stretcher bearer's back and out through his stomach. He seemed to turn green and was moaning in pain but still conscious; he was taken off to the RAP where he died several hours later.

From every direction came cries of wounded men, not by any means all of them British. If a slacker period came we hastily buried our dead though many laid unburied for several weeks. One evening there were terrible cries coming from the jungle to our right. Our men had found a method of dealing with the Japs by setting fire to the jungle and were mowing them down as they tried to escape.

I remained in this area until the early hours of February 15th. During this time I had to take my truck under heavy fire back to Battalion Headquarters (BHQ) for more ammunition and mortar bombs. Most of the time it was left under cover in front of our position and it was necessary to creep on my stomach to reach it.

It was while we were in this position we received a message of congratulation for holding on for so long; and also a promise that within two days the sky would be black with 'planes'.

It was – they were Japanese planes. Our only defence against them – rifle fire.

But the artillery supporting us put up the best show of fireworks I had ever seen. For three hours we could take our minds off our own situation and more or less watch the show, keeping our heads down when the shells seemed to be dropping too close to be healthy.

All this time the city of Singapore itself was being bombed heavily by groups of twenty seven and shelled by Jap artillery. We didn't know it until afterwards but the enemy took areas within the city boundary two days before capitulation.

Our flanks were exposed. We were on our own. Without withdrawing we carried on fighting.

Chapter 4

Burnt

"The soldier's trade, verily and essentially, is not slaying, but being slain."

John Ruskin

Sunday 15th February 1942. A day that time will never erase from my memory. Just before dawn, Sgt Holihead informed me that our mortar detachment was to move. I crawled to the truck to start the engine. When ready I signalled to the others, who reached the truck at the double. Where were we off to now? Two hundred yards down the road coils of danert wire barred our progress. We appeared to have been in front of our own front line! I slowed down and Sergeant Holihead hopped off the truck to clear the road. Although under fire all the time he held the wire back until I had driven through, then calmly replaced the wire and rejoined me in the front seat. It was hard to imagine a cooler man in action. Later he must have been blown to pieces as he was never heard of again after the cease fire.

We reached BHQ safely, things were a little quieter here, a hill on each side protected it from most of the fighting. There we hurriedly loaded up with more bombs and ammunition and, while the Sergeant was receiving further instructions, we endeavoured to find out how some of our pals had been faring. In return we gave news of what had been happening in our particular sector, names of men killed and wounded – Time for a quick smoke.

We drove to take up positions on another hill. Four other three inch mortar detachments were to be there too.

Battle strategy is seldom explained to the men doing the actual fighting, this was the case with us, we found out later that our battalion was now almost surrounded, our flanks were exposed.

We were to put up a barrage to cover the withdrawal of the battalion if need arose. At the bottom of the hill we left our trucks.

"You won't need those any more."

I didn't like the sound of this but there wasn't much time for thinking out the meaning of things. We manhandled all the ammunition and bombs from the trucks up the hill and dumped it in piles beside wooden huts and atap buildings. It was a long job and while it went on men were busy digging pits for the mortars, camouflaging them and generally getting prepared for the onslaught we expected to follow. During this time there was a certain amount of shelling and small arms fire but most of the enemy activity was in the air. We weren't being bombed but were undoubtedly being well observed from the low flying planes.

We had just about finished our task when the Sergeant sent me back to my truck to collect something he had left. I never got there. I had barely covered ten yards when I saw shells bursting all around the trucks. Perhaps I'd better wait a few minutes.

Crump! A shell fell near me. I made up my mind. I'd better wait!

I dived into the nearest trench. A Sergeant and Lance Corporal from 'A' Company were there already. Another Corporal followed me in. We were only just in time. Hell was let loose above us. The air seemed full of screaming hot metal. Everywhere men cried out as they were hit. Many being killed without time to make any sound. This couldn't last long, not more than half an hour. It could and did. Seemingly hours and hours. A shell landed among our mortar bombs, and one of the huts caught fire. Powerful explosions in addition to the normal barrage of shells and small arms fire followed. All our bombs seemed to be exploding. Surely it was impossible for anyone to remain above ground level and survive. A slight breeze quickly spread the fire through dry grass from hut to hut. All the hill was ablaze. An inferno of fierce crackling fire from burning grass and huts, it was impossible to see for flames and acrid smoke. The trench became like an incinerator, and all this time the Japs continued to plaster us with everything they had. It seemed suicidal to get out of the trench and make a dash for it; perhaps the fire would pass us, but it was obvious we couldn't remain in the trench much longer. Its sides were crumbling and falling in under the terrific vibration of the bursting shells. A blanket lay at the bottom of the trench, we held this over our heads to keep off the intense heat, it began to scorch. Now and again flames seemed to jump at us as though drawn by powerful magnets. We'd got to get out or be burned to death.

Burned to death. Yes, it looked like it. Oh! Ridley and Latimer! Candles not easily blown out! What was it my mother used to say about little boys who played with fire? Well, I could say this wasn't my fault.

The Sergeant was scrambling out. But the burns he received whilst doing so drove him back. He lost his nerve and fell back into the trench shouting "Help! We're burning to death!". There was no time for pity. The Lance Corporal scrambled out and was lost in the smoke and flames. The Sergeant and I were left. He hung on to me hysterically. I shoved him away. We would both burn to death if we delayed any longer. I was at the top of the trench. The flames licked at me. I saw the skin shrivel and peel off my hands and right arm. It was my arm. I didn't feel anything at the time.

A prayer "Oh God, let me get one quickly if I'm to die; don't let me burn to death." I'd been praying ever since the fighting started. So had the others; praying and asking, "Where's the RAF?"

Which way to run? I couldn't see. I was choking and had lost all sense of direction. I started to run in what I hoped was the direction of the Regimental Aid Post. Surely I wasn't running into enemy lines? The air seemed alive with screaming metal but I believed I was running out of the fire area. There was less smoke. Presently I was clear of the flames but my back was hurting like the devil. I must be on fire. That was it. My shirt was on fire. "Now what would one do with a person whose clothes are on fire?"

Memories of First Aid lectures when I was in the St John's Ambulance Brigade. Gaining a few more yards I rolled on the ground despite the pain it caused my back and hoped the flames were extinguished. Up again I staggered on until I found myself in the road near Battalion HQ. It was being heavily shelled. Trucks and houses were on fire. Utter chaos everywhere. I dropped into an anti-malarial drain where I found some of my pals. They did their best for me, covering my back with a gas cape and wrapping my hands and arms in handkerchiefs. The water truck was nearby and I gulped down at least four pints of water. They wouldn't let me drink anymore. They told me they never expected anyone to return from that hill of fire alive.

Jap tanks came down the road until halted by a direct hit from one of our mortars which was still firing. The tanks then started banging at us with their guns and my colleagues decided it was time I received treatment for my burns and two of them helped me towards the RAP. I collapsed every few yards but managed to recover each time until in the hands of the orderlies. They applied dry dressings and cotton wool pads to my back, burnt from neck to waist, and bandaged my hands, arms and left leg.

"You'll soon be comfortable in hospital," they assured me. This sounded fine. A comfortable bed, a pretty nurse, a trip home to England later on, perhaps. "How would you like to be in Royston now?" asked an Officer from my home town, as if reading my thoughts. He was suffering from a bullet wound in the face.

I had recovered enough to take notice of what was going on around me. The RAP was a private house. I had been taken upstairs and put beside other chaps on the floor. The first two I saw were the Corporal and Lance Corporal, my fellow occupants of the burning trench. They had been burned too and were bandaged like me. Shortly afterwards the Sergeant was brought in. His burns were worse than ours but he had recovered his nerve. I remember how pleased he was to see we were still alive. The poor devil died five days later in hospital.

What a shambles it was! Shell-shock cases were laughing and crying alternately; some were cracking jokes; some helping the hard-pressed orderlies; one chap fed me with pineapple chunks direct from a tin, plied me with whisky and gin, heaven knows where he got it, and helped me smoke a cigarette. Some men were saturated in blood and it was obvious they needed far more than first aid if they were to come out of this lot alive. No one displayed any sign of fear or panic. Perhaps because we were soldiers and experiencing nothing more than was to be expected in the heat of battle, but, more likely I suspect, because we were very young and even in these circumstances thought if death were to come to anyone, it would always be the other fellow, never us.

After about an hour an ambulance arrived and removed a number to hospital. We should go with the next lot we were told. When the next lot did arrive about an hour later the Japs were attacking very heavily and it was impossible for the ambulances to leave.

Chapter 5

Singapore Capitulates

"If our misfortunes were laid in a heap, whence everyone must take an equal portion, most persons would be content to take their own and depart."

Plutarch

Then came the news.

"At four thirty all British troops on the island will lay down their arms and surrender to the Japanese!"

We were thunderstruck, not knowing what to think. We could hardly believe our Commanding Officer when he came into the RAP and told us that. All of us were thinking of home – would we ever see England again? We'd heard stories of the way the Japanese treated their prisoners. In any case what Britisher wanted to admit to defeat by the Japs? But the CO had said we were not disgraced. He was pleased and proud of the way we had fought. He didn't want to give in.

But the lads didn't lay down their arms despite the order. They fought on more strongly than ever. But it was useless. Many lives were lost after the capitulation should have taken effect.

The fighting must have been at its peak soon after 6 pm when bullets came crashing through the windows of the RAP. The room where we were, seemed full of fallen plaster, dust and broken glass. A bullet struck the petrol tank of one of the ambulances outside. It immediately caught fire and before anything could be done the flames spread to the others. One of these was under the porch of the RAP and the building itself was soon burning fiercely.

The MO's, assisted by orderlies and other fit men, carried the wounded from downstairs up to our room. It seemed crazy to me. We should all be trapped.

Smoke began billowing up the stairs. Flames followed. I thought the end had come. After the burning trench, now this and there was no escape this time! By now I was barely conscious and events became very vague, but the Medical Officers knew what they were about. This house, like the others, was built on a slope and the room we were in opened on to the hill at the back. Someone had gone out with a large white sheet tied on a pole, the walking wounded next and the others were carried. Two chaps half carried me.

We were on a lawn at the back of the house and there were the Japanese. They were all over the place, hundreds of them, pointing rifles and light machine guns at us, grunting and gesticulating to everyone to put up their hands. I was thankful my arms were bandaged across my chest.

What small men they were? Loaded up with equipment, camouflaged from head to foot with small branches and bushes, they looked dirty in their ragged clothes and poor equipment, like walking bits of jungle.

But we were their captives! I could hardly believe it.

We were taken to a small drive about a hundred yards behind the RAP which was now blazing furiously. The roof had fallen in and it wasn't long before our Regimental Aid Post complete with medical supplies was razed to the ground.

In the drive our captors carried out a search, taking everything we possessed. Photographs, watches, rings and anything they fancied were grabbed from us. When this was finished we were taken to the lawn of another house a little further on and divided into three groups, officers, other ranks fit and wounded. Other prisoners joined us and Jap fighting troops seemed to be everywhere.

We must have presented a sorry sight, for five days and nights we had gone without food, sleep or washing and shaving. The Japs seemed afraid of us, they were so small compared with us, but their numbers gave them confidence. They gave cigarettes and water to the wounded. Some of the officers took photographs.

As men were being rounded up and brought to the area, many enquiries were made about pals:

"Have you seen Bill Jones?"

"He's OK but George Collins was killed yesterday and Bill Smith."

It was beginning to get dark when our CO made a short speech, thanking us for putting up such a good show, sticking together and fighting up to the end. He said he knew how we felt about capitulation. He felt the same but it was the civilian population and the failure of the water supply that had caused the surrender of the island. He said that the officers were being taken away from us but "Remember while you are prisoners you are still British. Hamper the Japs all you can." There were tears in the 'old boy's' eyes as he spoke, I thought he would break down.

We were then herded into a tennis court nearby. Not much larger than a single court with a very high wire surround. In this small area over 500 Cambridgeshires and half a dozen Suffolks waited for the next move while there were as many Japs outside to guard us.

It was well after dark when one of our officers returned with a Jap officer. They spoke together in Malay and the object of their discussion appeared to be the wounded lying at one end of the court. There wasn't room for other men to lie down, some sat, others were only able to stand. The upshot of the negotiation was that twenty of us who were wounded were carried into an upstairs room of the nearest house. Three men were carried to a different place. They were dead! Five medical orderlies came with us. Two Jap soldiers guarded the door, others were on the stairs and still more in the rooms below. I lay in the corner where I was placed, luckily on a mattress.

It seemed unbelievable. We'd surrendered to the Japs! Would our families at home know? What would they think? Perhaps they'd be getting information, "Missing, believed captured or killed", or perhaps they thought we were still in India.

By all the rules I should have had a restless night, but I was completely exhausted. I slept soundly.

Four and a half days we lived in that room and there was ample time to think. What a degrading state we were in. Two years training to fight an enemy and in less than a month we were prisoners. Filthy dirty, we hadn't washed or removed any of our clothes for well over two weeks. Now herded together, more than twenty men in one room, we would have found the smell revolting had we not far more pressing matters to occupy our minds. When, if at all, would we receive treatment for our wounds? We had heard that the Japs didn't take prisoners, but that after torturing them they finished them off with a bullet or a bayonet. At least, so far, we were still alive.

What was the situation in other parts of Singapore? We learned later that we were possibly the last battalion to cease fighting. Our record would stand scrutiny by anyone.

Our captors thought they had been fighting crack troops, an elite regiment. One of the finest in the British army. I understood they were convinced that our Commanding Officer was General Wavell and wanted to meet him.

Yes, it certainly was a miserable and unenviable situation. The British had capitulated and Singapore was in Japanese hands. It definitely was not the fault of the Cambridgeshires, we had fought to the bitter end.

What had those in responsible positions been doing in the years leading up to the invasion of Malaya and Singapore? Instead of taking elementary and necessary precautions to safeguard British interests and those of the civilian population, had those in authority been socializing and spending their time propping up bars in the Raffles Hotel and elsewhere?

I rather suspect they had.

Had we as members of the 18th Division been sacrificed in order that time might be gained in another theatre of war? Or for some other strategic ploy? Perhaps. Why didn't we have the support of the RAF?

Our thoughts were made up of many un-answered questions, but in spite of our troubles we were far better off than the chaps in the tennis court.

Our orderlies were allowed to scrounge food in the remainder of the house. Rations of two or three army biscuits with a small portion of bully beef or tinned fish were washed down with water taken from an anti-malarian drain in which lay the body of a Malayan. Nobody seemed any the worse for it. We were naturally always very thirsty and hungry.

From the window of our little confinement I could watch what happened in the tennis court. Once or twice a day biscuits and bully beef were thrown over the wire by the guards. Very little in proportion to the numbers, and men under heavy escort were allowed out to fetch water. They got it from the same source that we did. And only one man caught dysentery!

It incensed us to see the Japs pile food on the altar they had erected below our window. At sunrise and sunset they chanted prayers while we told each other what we could do with the bully beef and bananas on the altar. They seemed a crazy lot. As we watched them riding round the place on children's cycles and other toys we often asked ourselves, "How on earth did we lose to this gang?"

The question of latrines became a problem. The chaps outside scratched holes in the ground at one end of the tennis court and used them. The stench must have been disgusting in that heat.

It was, the guarding Japs were unable to stand the nauseating stink, they progressively moved their machine gun positions a little farther away.

We were taken under Jap escort by an orderly into the back garden where a hole in the ground served for us. It was a job to explain to the Japs what we wanted to do. I recalled how the previous night I had told of my urgent need to answer nature's call. This explanation by gesture to the Jap guard of what my trouble was seemed funny even then.

War brings strange experiences and I remember saying to my helper, a slightly wounded Lieutenant, "I never expected to have my backside wiped by a British Officer!"

As all the medical gear had been destroyed in the burnt out RAP we received no attention and our bandages had to stay put. How some of the men endured it I can't imagine. Pieces of shrapnel and bullets still in their bodies. I remember one man had been shot through the throat and every time he tried a little drink, the water ran out of a hole in his neck. My right arm was bad enough. It ached all the time and gave me so much pain, it seemed likely to burst through the bandages. The orderly removed them and revealed the whole hand and wrist covered by a large blister, more than an inch deep in places, it was very heavy and wobbled like greengage jelly as I moved my arm. There was no alternative but to replace the old dressing, tie the bandage loosely round it, and hope we should soon be sent somewhere for treatment.

We constantly enquired of our guards, "When will we go to hospital or at least receive medical treatment and supplies?"

They didn't know a thing, I don't suppose they understood us in any case.

On the fifth day two of their officers came and announced we were all going to a concentration camp at Changi, which was about twenty miles away. We were to march there. Men who couldn't march would be carried by those who could.

Walking wounded, who could manage it, hobbled downstairs into the road. The men were brought out from the tennis court and we were formed into a column, wounded in front, then the officers followed by the men. Ahead of us swaggered a Japanese officer. He couldn't have been more than five feet tall and his long sword trailed on the ground as he strutted along. As we marched the extent of the damage became apparent to us; overturned and burnt out vehicles were everywhere; buildings were in ruins, telephone wires and debris of all sorts abounded. From the bodies of the dead, flies swarmed up in thousands with a large buzz as we passed. In the more populous part of Singapore Japanese flags seemed to be hanging from every window, door and tree. The natives looked pleased enough at the Jap victory, or perhaps the defeat of the British. They all appeared to be waving little miniature Japanese flags. Any of them that got in the way, however, were knocked over by the little officer's sword or a Japanese rifle butt.

We marched, walked or staggered several miles in the broiling sun. A halt was called and we were allowed to rest in the shade of some trees. While we were resting our MO noticed a number of ambulances being driven by British personnel, free of Japanese escort, and asked the Japanese officer to stop one in order to get the wounded to hospital. An ambulance driven by an Indian was stopped and seven of our wounded were put in. The rest of us needing treatment boarded a fifteen hundredweight truck abandoned nearby and one of our fit MT drivers took the wheel. He was told to follow the ambulance. He did his best but the Indian drove very fast and we soon lost him. We decided to find a hospital ourselves but drove around for about half an hour without finding one. Japanese soldiers were everywhere, but they didn't interfere with us.

We didn't see any other British troops, where were they all? We hadn't been fighting the war on our own.

It all seemed very strange and unreal. We might not have been their prisoners at all. At one time we found ourselves at the water's edge. Here quite a number of sailing and motor boats had been left unattended. But it was madness to think of escape with only one fit man among us and not having the faintest idea where we were.

We turned round and drove back determined to stop the first ambulance we saw and somehow get to hospital.

Our luck was in. The first ambulance was in the charge of two members of the Royal Army Medical Corps (RAMC), who told us to follow them. We did, and soon found ourselves at a lunatic asylum for Asiatics.

It was a crazy world, but the authorities there said there was nothing they could do and told the RAMC men to take us to Alexandra Military Hospital. They, however, were in no hurry.

One brought out a crate of beer and spirits, the other opened the back of the ambulance and started playing a piano he'd got in there! What an unreal situation this was, we had been fighting for what seemed ages, shut up in a room for five days without treatment for our wounds or even a wash, and here were a couple of lunatics wanting to give us a piano recital. We weren't in the mood for a smoking concert and demanded to be taken to hospital immediately. This shook our would-be hosts who transferred four of our men to their ambulance and told our truck driver to follow.

All went well for a few miles until our truck ran out of petrol on a road by the side of which thousands of Japanese troops were camping. They crowded round our vehicle but didn't attempt to interfere with us. They appeared to be more curious than aggressive. An English speaking officer came along and I explained we were wounded men wanting to get to hospital and had run out of petrol. He seemed mystified until I kicked the petrol tank by way of illustration. His face lit up, "Ah Gasolene. OK". OK belonged to the universal language as far as the Japanese were concerned. He had one of his men bring eight gallons and we filled the tank but the engine wouldn't start. By this time the ambulance had returned so we decided to abandon the truck and pile into the ambulance, piano and all.

It was a nightmare journey. The driver raced along dodging shell holes and debris and we eventually reached Alexandra Military Hospital. An orderly came out and spoke to the driver. We heard him say something about the Japs shooting and bayoneting wounded as they lay in their beds. This was enough to send one of our number into fits of screaming and shouting. None of us were feeling too good at this news. This atrocity had taken place several days before the cessation of hostilities we were assured, but we couldn't be admitted.

How much more were we expected to take? Was everyone mad? Here we were, at long last, at the door of a Military Hospital and no one wanted to let us in. However, we were not going to be denied treatment this time. We refused to be turned away.

Being the senior member of our small party I was taken to the RAMC Colonel in charge, who upon hearing my story ordered that we be taken in, fed, washed and treated. We created a great deal of interest to all the medical staff, as indeed we had been doing wherever we went.

It appeared the hospital had not received any wounded for six days, they were surprised to see us arrive, filthy dirty, unshaven, wounds untreated and ravenously hungry. The fighting had ceased five days ago. Where had we been? It looked as though some other units hadn't fared so badly, most had already gone to Changi.

I had an operation when all the burned skin was removed from my body. It was grand to come round again and find myself in clean pyjamas between clean sheets. Looking round I saw my companions in the truck. How different they all were.

The Medical Officer thought it miraculous that we had gone so long without treatment. None of us had collected further complications in spite of our ordeal.

In the week or so we stayed at Alexandra Hospital the place was gradually cleared and all the patients sent to the Changi area. We were shown the wing where the Japs had slaughtered wounded men, doctors and orderlies. Very little could have changed since the event, blood-stained mattresses and sheets were still very much in evidence on some of the beds. We were told that Indian troops had taken cover in the Hospital and fired at the advancing troops, who, when they forced their way in, sprayed the place with bullets and bayoneted the wounded in their beds.

One orderly had a bayonet shoved in his back which went right through his body and came out of his chest. When I saw him he was walking about the ward with pieces of adhesive plaster back and front, apparently none the worse for his experience. He told me that when the Japanese troops came into the ward he was standing facing away from them. He felt a blow on his back and thought he had been struck by some heavy object. He was not aware of exactly what had happened until the Japanese soldier who dealt the blow, apparently unable to comprehend why the man hadn't fallen, but was still on his feet, peered round at the orderly's chest to see if he had lost his bayonet. The orderly, looking down to the area where the Jap was examining, saw to his horror an inch or so of steel sticking through. He promptly fainted.

Our meals were very scanty, out of tins, but not too bad what there was of it, a great deal better than we'd had over the past two weeks or so and, although we didn't know at the time, a gourmet's delight compared with what our diet would be in the future.

While in the hospital I managed to get a daily wash and shave with the help of a pal from my unit, he'd been shot through the buttocks but could still get about and use his hands. When taken prisoner the only clothes I had were those I stood in, but before leaving the hospital I made up some of my deficiencies with the help of this pal. He scrounged items belonging to chaps who had died, and I now had boots, socks, shorts, shirt, bush hat, blanket, pyjamas, mess tin, knife, fork, spoon and a towel.

In addition to these basic essentials I now possessed a small New Testament, active service edition, given to me by the hospital padre. It had a message from His Majesty the King in the front which ended, "and it behoves us in these momentous days to turn with renewed faith to this Divine source of comfort and inspiration." Very appropriate in the circumstances.

I left with the last men travelling by ambulance to Changi. An uneventful journey, we had no escort but were frequently stopped and searched by Japanese troops. After passing through several road blocks we eventually reached Changi where I was put in the surgical block of Roberts Hospital.

Conditions here were much different from those I had left. We were crowded together, the MO's and orderlies were terribly overworked, they didn't have the time to treat men as they would have wished. Our diet was changed to rice, this would be our food from now on. Twelve ounces a day was to be our ration, so we were told. Recollections of rice puddings at home made this seem not unpleasant until I had my first meal of boiled rice and salt, barely enough to cover a saucer.

By this time I was visited by some of my pals from our unit, they told me several hundred of them were in a few wooden buildings

New Testament given to me in Alexandra Hospital by a Padre, the only article, apart from my identity discs, to survive the whole period of captivity.

Singapore Capitulates

Photographs of the inside of the New Testament, I resisted the temptation to use the pages as cigarette papers and instead entered names and addresses of fellow POW's who I hoped to contact upon my return home. As they died I marked the entries with a small '✝'.

and tents, about three hundred yards from Roberts Hospital. They said they were supplementing their rice with tinned stuff, which they had looted and scrounged on the way from the tennis court. This decided me to get out of hospital as soon as I could, and by worrying the MO daily, he discharged me after twelve days. This on condition I reported twice daily to have my wounds dressed.

Out of hospital, I was able to fully realise, for the first time that we were prisoners of war. The Japs had enclosed us in an area about three miles square, two sides of which was the sea, and the remainder barbed wire. Except for a patrol twice a day we seldom saw our captors. Discipline was maintained by our own officers. Although there were many stone and wooden buildings in Changi, our battalion the 1st Cambridgeshires or what was left of it, was under canvas in a sand pit. Our period in the tennis court had caused us to be the last to arrive! We had to take what was left, not much reward for our determined stand, still is anything fair in war?

On one side of the area was a coconut grove and swamps, two sides the road, complete with barbed wire, and on the other the military cemetery. In the first two months three or four men a day were buried there.

For a few weeks all the work we did was for ourselves, digging latrines, collecting firewood and generally keeping the camp clean. Our own cooks prepared the meals and they did everything with rice except cook it, but, until the supply of tinned food ran out, the meals were just about edible. The rice diet soon began to cause stomach troubles, some men would be constipated for several weeks, while most found that the call of nature seemed never to let up. Our bladders constantly needed relieving, and to add to our misery, the normal warning signs of our natural needs, appeared to have deserted us.

It was in April, just when I no longer needed bandages, that I fell victim to this illness myself. I was soon doubled up with violent stomach pains, visiting the latrine every half hour and became light headed.

They carried me back to Roberts Hospital on a stretcher, I had got dysentery.

For the first few days in Roberts dysentery ward I was too ill to observe much of my surroundings. In those early days, our Medical Officers had experienced very little practical knowledge of the tropical diseases they were having to combat. The treatment they attempted to administer would be strictly in accordance with their medical training, but with precious little medicine and drugs at their disposal. As the time went on they became more competent and expert, often using all manner of unorthodox means of treatment with a great deal of success. When I went in, the standard treatment for dysentery, was to starve the patient for several days, at the same time giving him plenty of salts, until all traces of blood and mucus were gone from his motions.

Like everyone else, I had my "magsulp" (magnesium sulphate) three times a day, and as much slightly salted water as I could drink. Nothing to eat, but in any case I felt too ill to want food. The pain continued and my visits to the latrines averaged about twenty times during the day, and slightly more at night for the first three or four days. The latrines were pails and tins placed at one end of the ward. Not a very comfortable place to spend one's time. Two of the pails had loose wooden seats, but there was never much time to make a choice, and usually very difficult to find a vacant bucket. Once a day we had to supply a small sample in a tin lid, for microscopic examination.

After a few days I was too weak to visit "smell row" and became a bed patient, shouting for a bed pan at frequent intervals. Six days went by and the MO thought I might be able to take a little food. He put me on a light diet.

Light diet at home perhaps meant a lightly boiled egg, and tasty bread and butter with the crusts cut off, perhaps a little tasty soup. Light diet here consisted of a little unappetising rice and some vegetable water. I couldn't eat it, and it was at this time I had my first encounter with the "human hawks". These were chaps possessing large appetites, just getting back on their food. They couldn't get enough to eat, and used to patrol round waiting to devour the rice of the men who were unable to take it.

After ten days I was put on a full diet, which was the same as light but more of it. It was terrible stuff, but I did manage to get a few mouthfuls down each meal-time. Everytime I saw the stuff I nearly vomited, but I was rapidly learning that however one felt, the rice had to be forced down, even when it seemed impossible, the only alternative was death.

By this time I was on my feet again, my visits to "smell row" were far less frequent, and I was able to take stock of my surroundings. Roberts Hospital was originally army barracks, it only became a place for the sick when all the prisoners were concentrated at Changi. It consisted of five or six stone buildings, each containing three floors.

One block would be surgical, one malaria, another dysentery

etc. I was on the centre floor of the dysentery block, sleeping on the balcony with a stretcher for my bed. The floors were designed to accommodate thirty men, now each housed more than a hundred, some on stretcher beds like me, but many directly on the concrete floor.

The MO's seemed to have a free hand, no Japs visited here, they were too frightened of catching disease. Most men were staggering about like skeletons, and there were at least two deaths each day in this ward. To me it was a terrible place but proved to be a palace, compared with some of the so-called hospitals I was to experience later.

By the end of three weeks I was eating much better and actually beginning to feel hungry. The MO said I could return to my unit. I didn't need to be told twice. I gathered up my meagre possessions, eager to get away from this atmosphere of sickness, and back to my friends in the sand pit.

"Blimey, you look skinny," they said. Someone produced a valuable possession – a mirror. Looking into it I was shocked at the change. Surely this wasn't me, my cheek bones stuck out, my eyes sunken in, I had certainly lost weight and to make things worse I badly needed a shave. Borrowing a razor from someone, still lucky enough to possess one and a few blades, I soon changed my appearance. It was good to be back.

My appetite increased daily and I ate anything I could. Any rice left over, after the main queue had been served, was offered to us who were very thin. After eating my normal ration, I could usually eat another helping of plain rice and thoroughly enjoy it. I began to put on weight, although it was only what we had come to call "rice fat". My losses from dysentery were not going to be replaced by plain rice. Life for the next month in our sand pit could not be described as arduous. We did a little work in the morning, and spent the rest of the day playing cards or talking. The main topic of conversation was usually food, we were always hungry and most used to dream about it at night. We had two meals a day, breakfast was usually a small helping of sweetened and plain rice, the evening meal rice and stew, watery vegetable stuff with no trace of vegetables except sometimes the odd floating piece of pumpkin. Twice a week the stew had a faint flavouring of meat and the cooks attempted making a rissole or pastie.

Chapter 6

River Valley

"Doubtless the pleasure is as great of being cheated, as to cheat. As lookers-on feel most delight, that least perceive a juggler's sleight, and still the less they understand, the more th' admire his sleight of hand."
                                                                Samuel Butler

It must have been May, when a hundred of us were picked to go to River Valley. We had been paraded, and the MO selected those he thought were the fittest men. I wasn't sorry to be reckoned among them. It seemed to me that a change of scene and occupation would relieve the tedium of imprisonment. Many of the chosen party had either no boots or very badly worn ones, so all men not going were paraded too and had to give up or exchange boots with us. We were told that we were to march to River Valley, but need carry nothing more than our mess tins, as lorries would take the rest of our stuff.

I was pleased to have with me, Reg Darlow and George Wright, two chaps from my home town, Royston Herts, as we set off early in the morning. At Changi boundary we were taken over by Japanese escort and the real march began. It was very hot, and before long we were very tired and thirsty. The Japs were fairly decent and didn't hurry us too much, they allowed us several rests on the way. All the same, when we reached Singapore city we were gasping for drink, and were glad of the water that Chinese and other natives offered us. We walked until it was dark, and then were told there was one more mile to go. I was exhausted. Six months earlier I would have laughed at this march, but now I could barely stand.

Eventually we reached our destination, and were halted near a Japanese guard room where we were counted dozens of times.

My identity discs and a 'lucky elephant' which I found in a deserted house in Singapore. The wooden number replaced the cloth AP135, of River Valley, at a later date.

When the guards were satisfied about the numbers we were bundled into a wooden hut. The officer in charge discovered that a meal had been prepared for us by POW's already in the camp, and we were astonished to receive as much rice as we wanted, with meat stew and sweet tea without milk. This was wonderful after Changi and many of us had the feeling of a full stomach for the first time for many weeks.

Next we had to find our kits in the dark and get down to some sleep, the wash could wait until morning. I received another shock however, the delight of the large meal was spoiled for six of us by the news that our kit had been stolen from the lorry after it had left Changi. How low could some POW's sink? Pinching perhaps the only means of survival from their fellow prisoners. All my possessions were what I stood up in, plus a mess tin and spoon! This was a bad start, but I laid down where I was, the mess tin for a pillow and was soon sleeping soundly.

I was awakened in the morning by the noise of men scrambling about clanging mess tins, they were queuing for breakfast, and I was not slow to join them. Again as much plain rice as one wanted and a spoonful of sugar to help it down. There were also cold showers to use, this again was an advance on Changi. We discovered that there were to be two roll calls a day, one in the morning at eight thirty and one in the evening at seven o'clock. We were to work from after the morning roll call until five in the evening with one hour break at mid-day.

The chap in charge of roll-calls was a Japanese private called Saito. He had his name on his tunic in English and Japanese. He was small and wore spectacles and we never saw him except at roll-call. He paraded us in fives, not the usual British army threes, apparently our captors could count more easily in fives. The first day was to be spent learning a few words of command in the Japanese language. Our guards found it very amusing trying to get us to respond to their orders, a shouted command and some of us would do one movement, others something entirely different. We learnt to number in Japanese, enough to get by at any rate, this early in our days of captivity. We received the order "Kotski" meaning attention, and then "Bango" for "Number" and away we went – "Itchi, Nee, San, See, Go" – one, two, three, four, five etc. Experience taught us that as long as the first few men shouted their number correctly, and the last one, having checked beforehand what his number should be, anything could be shouted in between. We supplemented Ace, Jack, Queen, King and anything that came to mind. It usually worked.

As time went on we naturally picked up more of their language, but only enough to suit ourselves, phrases to our advantage and keep us out of trouble. "Mukadumus Ni" became a useful phrase, it meant, "Do not understand". Our captors, of course, learnt some of the English language from us. It didn't usually resemble anything that might have been taught at a British University and caused us some degree of amusement during times when there would be little else to smile about. There would be nothing unusual to be told by a Jap that you were a " No pucking good bastard" a "Canaro buggaro" or simply that you were "no good ta na".

"Speedy Benjo" became very important words in our vocabulary, they implied that one was in need of dashing to answer nature's call in a hurry, as we frequently did later on.

"Yasumi" or "Yasme" which meant rest was the one word we never forgot and liked best of the Japanese language.

The following day we got down to the real reason for our being there. We had our farcical roll-call and after the numbers had been checked by Saito, seven or eight of his countrymen, little grinning devils in shabby uniforms, came along to take parties of us for work. It didn't take long to find out whose party it paid to be in, and we would scheme to get with the right man.

We became AP Company (Administrative Party) and were given

cloth numbers to wear on our hats or shorts, my number was AP132. It was about this time that we learnt to know the Japs as Nipponese, which meant that in future we always referred to them as 'Nips'.

River Valley camp was about three hundred yards long and two hundred wide. The camp was bordered on one side by a road and on the opposite side, a sluggish oily looking river, not deep enough to take any boats, in fact the water looked well nigh stagnant. On the other sides were areas of open land with the odd building here and there. The camp was surrounded by a high barbed wire fence, and in this compound probably twenty huts each housing about a hundred men. The showers were sited along the roadside of the camp, no privacy here, as we washed we were in full view of whoever might be passing a few yards on the other side of the wire.

Sometimes a Nip would return to camp in a rickshaw, often flat out drunk and I promised myself, as a post-war treat, to get one of the blighters between the shafts and make him run until he dropped.

Within the camp an English Colonel was in charge, and he had a staff of officers and an interpreter. There were about two thousand of us and we were split into working parties of about two hundred men in each with an officer in charge. The companies were made up of men from various units, our company consisted of Cambridgeshires, Royal Artillery, Ordnance Corps etc. POW Royal Army Service Corps (RASC) men received our rations and distributed them to the companies. Each company had four or five cooks, a Royal Army Medical Corps (RAMC) orderly, a Company Sergeant Major (CSM) and a clerk to keep account of any records and pay. Mine was twenty five cents a day at that time, sufficient to buy one packet of cigarettes, Chinese horrors, we called them, they were enough to blow one's head off. A much better buy was a small handful of peanuts.

Several sentry boxes were sited about the camp, and the sentries changed hourly. If a sentry was armed he had to be saluted. The only time other Nips entered the camp enclosure was for roll-call and taking charge of working parties.

The huts in which we lived were built of wood with atap roofs. There was a gangway down the centre, and on either side of it wooden platforms, one above the other, men sleeping in two tiers. Although I had one or two items given me to make up for what had been stolen, I slept every night in my old pair of shorts and shirt. I had nothing to cover me, and only an old piece of groundsheet to lie on. My hips and back became very sore at first, but hardened after a time. The huts were infested with bugs which started biting as soon as we laid down to sleep. Their attentions combined with the sticky heat, drove men to stand outside the huts in bright moonlight, which at the time of full moon made reading quite easy. The bugs looked like lady birds without the spots and could easily bite through cloth. We became expert at catching the revolting things, pinching them between finger and thumb they squashed like a ripe tomato, were full of blood and smelt of burnt almonds. These vermin were to be part of our existence for the next three years, together with lice, mosquitoes and many other unpleasant creatures.

The first job I had to do for these Nips was to collect the camp's rice ration from a store at the docks. There were eighty of us on this job and we were taken to the docks by lorry. Hundreds of sacks of rice had to be taken from the warehouse to the lorries, and it wasn't long before we found a sack of sugar among them, and helped ourselves pretty freely. All went well until two of our boys had the misfortune to be caught in the act, and then I witnessed my first Nip beating. They were knocked all over the store by the guards using fists and boots indiscriminately. But this didn't stop the rest of us pilfering. We noticed some small sacks of flour, and decided to pinch a few by putting one or two sacks on each truck, and covering them with sacks of rice. I remember knotting the ends of my shirt sleeves, and filling them with flour. Nothing seemed to have been noticed, and we had boarded the trucks ready to return to camp, when the Black Guards (Crack Nip Troops) came along and ordered us to get down. Of course after searching they found a lot of the loot and we were rewarded with beatings on the spot. Our faces were punched by a number of clenched fishes, and unprotected skins kicked repeatedly. Some of our booty escaped their vigilance however, and our camp supplies were increased, despite the Nips, who failed to find many places where we hid the stuff.

Later, on one trip to Singapore, we met a man who spoke English so well that we asked him what the devil he was doing, why had he not been interned? He explained that he was Irish and a neutral, and thus free to do as he pleased. As an illustration of this he bought us some pork sausages in the Chinese market.

Stealing became a passion with us, and a fine art. Whatever job we had to do our first consideration was, "What can we 'pong' (ie steal) that will be useful to us?" Twice a week, for example, we were taken to the cold storage in Singapore to fetch meat and potatoes, and invariably we were successful in distracting the guard's attention while we loaded an extra side of meat or sack of potatoes. We worked this trick on several occasions but thought that the game was up one day when the guard checked the sides of meat on the journey back to camp. He counted them several times, and looked very puzzled until suddenly, a look of understanding came into his eyes. Grinning broadly he said, "Mukadimus", meaning understand, and explained in half Japanese, half English, that he had no objection to this sort of thing, provided we shared with him on a fifty-fifty basis. He made it plain, that if we were caught, he would know nothing about it. On this understanding we did quite well for ourselves, with this Nip, on subsequent occasions.

Ours wasn't the only racket in the camp; foodstuffs and tobacco were bought outside from Malays or Chinese, smuggled in and sold inside at a tremendous profit. Of course they ran a risk, and the lads wanted the stuff hence the business flourished. In defence of our "ponging" it can be said that the results of it benefited a greater number than those of us involved in the actual deed. My pal said to me, "I shall warn my parents never to allow you in their shop when we get home." I think this was after the incident of the bars of soap. I was in a gardening party when I had to return the tools to the Nip billets, where they were stored. Inside the hut were bars of soap, about twenty inches long. Now soap was just what we needed. The scanty ration the Nips allowed went nowhere. Perhaps I should say that later on there were no issues at all. However, I saw to it that I returned the tools, after the next gardening fatigue and, this time, I went armed with a piece of string. It didn't take me long to grab a bar of soap, cut it in two with the string, and suspend a piece down each leg of my shorts. As soon as I got back to my hut, the soap was cut into pieces the size of the Nip ration, and distributed so that if any search was made, each of us could claim that it was an issue. This continued as long as the soap lasted and after supplies ran out I got myself on to another party.

One day two of us came across a bottle on a shelf in a Nip billet. Of course we couldn't read the Japanese label, but we agreed that the contents must be vitamin tablets, so we consumed the bottleful between us on the spot! Whatever they were they did us no harm, or good, for that matter. How weak I was had been brought home to me when I needed help to climb on to the back of the lorry.

The Nip in charge of the gardening was known to us as "Dysentery Dick", for the good enough reason that he made us collect the contents of the latrines, take it in large drums to gardens outside the camp, and empty it on to his plants.

Another Nip we called "Bull Frog", because we thought he looked like one, he sounded like one too. He was quite a harmless, almost likeable fellow really, and looked as though he must have some Negro blood in his veins. These bull frogs, the animal ones that is, gathered near the water and damp ground and used to make a terrific noise at night grunting and groaning like snorting pigs.

Dysentery Dick would leave us to work two or three hours at a time, while he went to see his girlfriend who lived nearby. This suited us fine and there was very little work done in his absence. Many a time he sent me to fetch his container of tea, and I soon discovered how to make this journey profitable. When I received the tea, I would grimace at the Nip cook and say with many signs, "He say, Satunika, no sugar". Whereupon a bowl of sugar was forthcoming for Dysentery Dick. I need not say that he never got it!

Not all the civilian population could have been co-operating with the Nips. While in River Valley, we heard of some sort of trouble they had caused, and on one of our truck journeys to work, we saw how ruthless the Nips could be. A number of severed heads had been stuck on poles, with notices underneath, presumably as a warning to other natives to behave themselves.

Even apart from our stealing the little extra that meant so much, the food at River Valley was quite the best I had as a prisoner. At this time the Nips allowed larger rations to working men, and there were always the little extra meals we prepared ourselves.

Never a night went by when there wasn't a little group of men to be seen, squatting round a fire cooking their spoils, in home-made or stolen cooking utensils.

Most of the Nips in River Valley turned a blind eye to these cooking sessions, in fact, the only serious crime that came to my notice during my period there, was the striking of a prisoner on the head with a bayonet scabbard. He died in hospital and the Nip who caused his death was hastily removed from the camp.

At this time the likelihood of freedom seemed very remote. We heard the news broadcasts from New Delhi radio through a wireless set in one of the cookhouses. It was well hidden, and switched off at the approach of any Nip. We knew how serious the war situation was, and the Nips never tired of telling us we wouldn't return home, but spend the rest of our days as their slaves. One Nip offered to take me to Japan, when the war was over, and make me his chauffeur at the princely wage of four shillings a week. Later on, when our lot became very much worse, we often looked back with envy to the River Valley days.

Every Thursday was "Yasumi" day when we did no work except for ourselves. We used to spend the time improving our living quarters. We scrounged sacks, wood, nails, borrowing a saw from one place and pinching a hammer from another. My two pals and I built ourselves a bed each, arranged them U shape with a table in the middle. We made a lamp from a tin and piece of rope and used paraffin stolen from a Nip cement mixer. We called this "Imperial Palace" and in the evenings would sit round our table in the light of the lamp, drink our five cents worth of tea, smoke a "dog end" and talk of home.

In June 1942 we wrote our first cards, the Nips issued them and we were told we could write what we liked.

"I don't suppose they'll reach England but I'd better write."

"I'm sending mine to Churchill. He'll like to know how we are after getting us into this bloody mess."

Many didn't bother to write cards. They argued it was only a waste of time as the Nips would never send them off. One chap did write to Churchill, and asked to be remembered to Peter Gurney, Ian Stuart and Uncle Tom Cobley and all. On returning to the United Kingdom, I discovered that some of these first cards did reach their destinations about a year later. Subsequent cards were in printed form and had a choice of messages to send or cross out. I sent five cards in all during my period of captivity.

Perhaps the climatic conditions in which we worked and existed in River Valley are worth mentioning, the same would apply anywhere in Singapore. The temperature remains more or less constant the whole year round, it is usually about ninety degrees Fahrenheit in the shade, a sticky damp heat with very little change at night. At mid-day it is frequently one hundred and thirty degrees in the sun. We worked in shorts only and sweated continuously. At night sleep was difficult because of the heat. Rain always came in the form of a storm, the wind would suddenly increase, almost as abruptly slacken, and down would come the rain. Absolutely teem down, but within an hour it would all be over and once more the sun would blaze through, the atmosphere become oppressive, humid and with no breeze at all.

So many little things normally taken for granted, are not missed until one has experienced having to do without them for long periods. The list was becoming almost endless, even so early in our spell as prisoners. Not having access to a pair of scissors, for example. I had learnt to bite off excess lengths of fingernail as a necessity, not as a habit, continuing the practice until my release. Toe nails were a different proposition. I couldn't adopt the same method for them, instead, when they became long enough, I would make a small nick on one side of the nail, and then pull or tear the unwanted piece from one side of the toe to the other. This generally produced a satisfactory result, but on one occasion, I had started the operation a little too low down, pulled the offending piece off, and the result of my carelessness, within a few days, was a painful ingrowing toe nail.

I had been as content here in River Valley, as it was possible to be in a Nip prison camp. It was, therefore, a great disappointment to me when, towards the end of July, reporting sick with that badly swollen toe, I was informed that I was being sent back to Changi. River Valley was not a place for men unable to perform a full day's work.

My last evening was spent in the "Imperial Palace" with my pals, George Wright and Reg Darlow, I wondered if I should see them again, I did, both of them. But George died later on and Reg Darlow I met in Royston after it was all over.

The next morning saw me off to Changi with my small bundle of kit, fifty cents (eight pence) in my pocket, travelling this time by truck under Nip escort.

Chapter 7

Changi

"There is a certain relief in change, even though it be from bad to worse; as I have found in travelling in a stage coach, that it is often a comfort to shift one's position and be bruised in a new place."
                                                    Washington Irving
                                                         1783-1831

Although I was not fit enough to work at River Valley, I was fit enough not to be detained in hospital when I got back to Changi, so I rejoined my unit. There were less than a hundred Cambridgeshires in our unit area now, but I was surprised to find how things had improved. A large hut had been built from odd pieces of wood, and the roof thatched with coconut palms. The majority slept in this. Only a few remained in tents, but they all had plenty of room. Nearly every man had made himself some sort of bed.

The meals were better too, although not as plentiful as at River Valley, they were a vast improvement on the food dished up when I was last there. There were now three meals a day, breakfast plain rice and a spoonful of sugar, mid-day, or tiffen as we came to call it, rice and light green water made from sweet potato tops. The evening meal brought a little more vegetable stew, still watery, but with the occasional chunk of pumpkin or marrow, and sometimes perhaps, the odd thread-like strand of meat.

There was so little salt at Changi that in our unit they were making their own, one man was being employed full-time boiling down sea water which parties of men collected in large oil-drums. Flour was a luxury of the past, but by grinding down the rice some baking was possible, using ovens made from oil drums and other containers. Some fertilizer had come to hand, and after a little experimentation it was mixed with rice, baked, and made quite edible food. The Battalion garden among the coconut palms, yielded small crops of onions, spinach, beans and sweet potato tops. Nearby another area had been cultivated, this was the Brigade garden; men from several units worked on this and the resultant crops distributed round the various battalions.

Men were certainly doing their best to improve their lot as prisoners. No outside work was being done. Below the rank of corporal the pay was ten cents a day, above fifteen cents. Officers I believe received much more. There was not much to buy at the little canteen that the Nips had allowed to be formed in the camp. Twenty cents was the price of a packet of Chinese cigarettes, thirty cents procured a pint of peanuts and forty-five cents a bottle of soya bean sauce. The sauce helped the rice down considerably, and I found I could make a bottle last twenty days if careful. I bought peanuts, which contained vitamin B, rather than the terrible cigarettes. Giving up smoking didn't hit me as hard as some. I've seen chaps follow an officer to pick up his fag end only to be disappointed. He was also short, and so the end was nipped out and put in his tin, and kept with others to roll into a cigarette later! Some men tried smoking tea leaves and many other things with little success!

Those of us that were well enough to do so, did our best to keep fit by PT and unarmed combat. Cricket was played on the Pedang, a large sports ground, several afternoons a week. England v Australia was always a popular match, with Barnet, an Australian test match player, appearing for his country to add the touch of seriousness. Some of the fitter men played football in the evenings, all the players wearing slippers or gym shoes.

A concert party was in full swing, and the shows ran for a fortnight at a time. Although these were presented twice nightly, it wasn't possible for everyone to see the shows, and seats were allocated to each section of the camp. They were good. Men played the parts of females of course, and did it extremely well. How long was it since we had seen a woman?

Church services were held on Sundays, and those of us interested used to smarten ourselves up as much as possible, to attend our particular denominational "Church". This usually consisted of an altar under a lean-to. The congregation sat on the ground in the open.

Everything was being done to help men endure the tedium of imprisonment, but by this time we were all looking pretty shabby. The clothing and footwear problem was becoming acute. My shirt and shorts were covered by different coloured patches, and my boots had long since worn out. There was no chance of renewing anything, I was wearing gym shoes. Practically everyone was in this state, at least we in the Cambridgeshires were. We had been made prisoners, as had many others, in close contact with the enemy, and, of course, had only what we were wearing at that time. There were, however, a number of units far more fortunate, not having had our experience, or at least being able to supplement their clothing shortages, before being sent to Changi. Officers who had not been in the thick of the action were not short of kit either, many still had most of their possessions, clothing, blankets, mosquito nets, odd bits of furniture, books etc. and money.

We could still get a little soap and washed our clothes as often as possible. We shaved by borrowing a razor from someone lucky enough to have scrounged one. The rice diet began to take its effect, and men began to suffer from all manner of vitamin deficiencies. Men had sore mouths and tongues, rough blotchy powdery skin, scrotum dermatitis, very unpleasant. We knew this by several different names, usually by the name of the camp in which it manifested itself. There were ulcers on the legs, ringworm and all manner of skin diseases, but nothing compared with what I would be seeing later.

The death rate in Roberts Hospital was about five a week at this time, dysentery, diptheria and malaria being the chief causes. Sick men were returning to Changi daily from working camps on the Island, Bukit Timor, and Singapore, the more serious going straight into hospital, but the majority going back to their units to become, "sick in lines".

Changi had been wired off into several areas, and to pass from one to another we had to be marched past the sentry by an officer carrying a flag with a Nip device on it. The sentries between these areas were Sikhs who had deserted to the Nips. Sentries had to be saluted and would often strike a man for an improper salute. It made us fume, but there was little that could be done about it, although a couple were killed one night and shoved head-first into the holes bored for latrines.

Several parades were held on the roadside. We were made to line the roads, and stand for ages, until a number of high ranking Nips passed by, and propaganda photographs were taken. After one of these parades all officers, above the rank of Lieutenant Colonel, left us. We heard they were going to Japan.

Chapter 8

Selarang

"None but the Guilty can be completely miserable . . ."
                                                    Goldsmith

It was early September 1942 when we heard that the Nips were issuing orders that all prisoners must sign forms promising not to escape. We were paraded by our officer. He explained the situation, "What do you think about it chaps? Do you intend to sign?"

"No."

We were British soldiers. It was our duty to escape if we could. It was also our duty to make things as difficult as possible for our captors. Under our Military Law, and we were told, all International Law, such an assurance should never be asked for or given. To make it perfectly plain to us we were paraded several times, but the answer was always the same. No!

Then in the early hours of the morning we were paraded once more. We were told to collect our kit and odds and ends together as quickly as possible; we were being sent to Selarang Barracks. What was to happen to us we had no idea, most of us didn't even know where Selarang was, but we did know we were being concentrated there for refusing to sign the forms.

Selarang Barracks was the former home of a Scottish Battalion. There were eight blocks on the sides of the square, three down two of the sides, two on the third and several small buildings on the fourth, the whole area being about two hundred yards by two hundred and fifty yards. A road ran round the outside of the block, this was strictly out of bounds, any men found on it would be shot.

There were only two roads into Selarang which, by the time our unit's turn came to move, were congested beyond belief. The refugees from Malaya had nothing on our trip to Selarang. The distance was less than two miles but it took several hours to cover it. We were packed in the road like a lot of ants. Men carried their meagre belongings in sacks, some on their heads, others on poles. Some men were hung around with cooking pots and pans, while others carried ducks, chickens, beds and musical instruments. One man, a sergeant known as Snowy, about whom more will be said later, was completely smothered from head to foot with all manner of gear, gadgets and odds and ends. God knows where he had accumulated it all from, but it was amazing that he was able to stagger along at all. Still Snowy was quite a character at any time, in any event.

There were a number of trucks from which the Nips had removed the engines, these, pushed by eight or so men were laden with all manner of cooking gear, complete home made ovens and rations that had not yet been consumed.

The allocation of the small space that Selarang provided was carried out by our own officers. Our unit, the 1st Cambs was allocated the top floor of one of the blocks and this was to be shared with the remnants of three other battalions and Brigade HQ. There was no room to move. We were like thousands of bees swarming the Queen. It took nearly an hour to reach our floor as the stairway was completely blocked with struggling bodies. Once we reached our allotted space there was no room except to stand. Troops were packed shoulder to shoulder like sardines, sweating sticky bodies everywhere. Some of us climbed up a rope ladder through a trap door in the ceiling and let ourselves out on the flat roof. It wasn't long before we were joined by others, but crowded though we became it was far better than the packed mass of bodies on the floor below.

Looking round the blocks we could see that we weren't the only ones to fancy a roof top position; in fact some on other buildings had even rigged up tents for themselves. Airy though our position was, it soon became obvious that it had disadvantages of inaccessibility. We had to descend sometimes. To get down took half an hour! Thirty minutes to travel forty feet!

That night we heard from our CO that the Nips intended to keep us in Selarang until we signed the "Non escape" forms.

They hoped to starve us into submission, no rations would be issued and anybody stepping outside the concentrated area, or even approaching the barbed wire which now encircled us, would be shot. Machine guns were mounted at frequent intervals, Sikhs and Nip troops manned these and also patrolled the perimeter. It wasn't a cheerful prospect. Luckily, unknown to us, our cooks had built up a reserve of rations in the event of such an emergency and it was thought we should be able to get two meals a day. One pint of water per man was to be the daily allowance for all purposes.

After some sort of sleep under the stars, we woke in the morning to survey the scene afresh. The view from the roof was an incredible sight. Nearly eighteen thousand men crammed in an area built to accommodate eight hundred and fifty. Tents, ground sheets, gas capes and all manner of things were stretched out as make shift covering. There were absolutely no sanitary arrangements. Latrines were hastily being dug by large parties of men, they had worked consistently throughout the night digging trenches about fourteen feet deep in the middle of the parade ground. Snake-like queues of men desperately needing to relieve themselves, stretched for hundreds of yards, although perhaps no more than fifty yards, in a direct line, away from their ultimate objective. It took about an hour to reach the latrine after getting into a queue. Needless to say delay in joining the queue brought unpleasant results for the unfortunate victim, and more fodder for the carriers of dysentery and disease.

On the other side of the coin, taking so long to reach one's destination often meant no satisfactory result on arrival. Officers and privates squatted together, cheek by jowl. No time for rank distinction or modesty here! The stench was atrocious and flies swarmed everywhere.

Despite all the difficulties the cooks managed to prepare some sort of meals, doors and cupboards were torn down to make the necessary fires.

We had pep talks from our CO. He told us that it was our duty not to sign and asked us if we were prepared for the consequences. We were told how four recaptured men had been shot in Changi gaol. One man was shot three times before he was killed. The first shot got him in the arm and he called out, "Come closer you bastards and you might be able to hit me!" At the second shot he fell to the ground where the third one finished him. Despite all this we were determined not to sign. Surely they would never kill us all. "No" was still our answer. Some chaps thought the Nips intended to make us sign forms and then drop them as leaflets over Britain.

"How the hell are they going to fly to England?" asked another.

"They can send them to Germany and get the Nazis to do it for them, can't they?" was the immediate reply.

On the roof with me was "Mabel" and he provided us with about the only amusing incident of our ordeal. On my return from

CHARLES THRALE

This drawing, by Charles Thrale, goes a long way to illustrate the Selerang Incident, where 18,000 of us were herded into a confined area, without rations, for refusing to sign 'Non Escape' forms. Note prisoners forming queues for hurriedly-improvised latrines.

River Valley I had been put in charge of a tent in which one of the occupants was "Mabel". He was a girlish sort of chap, hence his nickname. Because of his nature he was the butt of everybody's jokes and seemed to get a raw deal in everything. Feeling sorry for him I made it my business to see that a lot of the leg-pulling ceased, and because of this became quite a friend to him. I learned quite a lot about his past. He had no one in the world to care whether he returned home or not. His only relative was a sister who had impounded his savings. He had made the journey from Changi with us, and when I decided to sleep on the roof nothing would satisfy him but that he had to come too. His performance trying to climb the rope ladder with his kit had to be seen to be believed. He would get a few feet off the floor and end up with his legs pointing towards the ceiling, giggling like a girl the whole time. Eventually we had to drag him feet first through the trap-door onto the roof. All in the vicinity were doubled up with laughter which increased when Bolder, the sergeant in charge of the buglers, bawled up telling him to get his scanty kit, and the bugle, he still possessed, and report to the temporary HQ.

"What's it all about?" asked "Mabel".

"Oh, it's a cushy job," shouted Bolder. "You will sleep in the HQ while we're here and blow a few calls when required."

Then came the comic turn of "Mabel's" descent. It was as much trouble to get him down as it had been to get him up and his giggling and our laughter didn't help much. Eventually he got down and made his way to the Emergency HQ, proud to be wanted for such an important job. Half an hour later there was the most hideous and discordant noise, something like a cow bellowing in mortal agony.

"What in the name of Tojo is it?" It was repeated several times and caused quite a discussion.

"Surely that's never a bugle?"

It was! It was Mabel mixing every call there was in one grand fantasia of his own and we were not in the least surprised, a little later on, when commotion below warned us that "Mabel" had been fired, and was ready to re-join us. We went through the pantomime on the rope again and "Mabel" was dragged, kit, bugle and all onto the roof once more. When his giggling had subsided he announced: "I'm a bit out of practice, I just blew 'All Officers' and they gave me my ticket!"

For three days, in appalling conditions, we remained in Selarang, barely able to move, packed in like sardines, hungry, sweating and filthy, keeping up our spirits as best we could with sing-songs and jokes. The Nips couldn't shoot us all, could they? But we didn't think too much. It was enough to still be alive.

Then the blow fell. Disease had broken out, there had been several deaths and it was likely more would follow. Furthermore the Nips had ordered that all the occupants of Roberts Hospital were to be brought into Selarang. All of them, limbless men, malaria, dysentery and diphtheria patients and all. This would mean death for hundreds of them, and us, and the Senior Officer in charge of all POW's had ordered every man to sign the "Non Escape" form. He assured us that he would be entirely responsible for our signing, it was a direct order from him which we must obey and there would be no stain on our character as soldiers. He had also procured a document from the Nips saying that we had signed under extreme duress. We were assured that we could always break our promise if the opportunity arose. We were reluctant to sign, but our own CO pointed out that this was an order from the highest ranking British Officer in Singapore and refusal to sign would cause many deaths.

The forms were on the spot and we all signed, Bill Jones signing as Tom Smith and Tom Smith signing as Bill Jones. The Nips had our names and numbers and would have been able to check with the "Non Escape" forms to their own satisfaction had they chosen to, but we had eased our consciences by the knowledge that we had not really signed a promise to refuse to escape.

As soon as the forms were signed the wire was taken down, the barriers removed and we were on our way back to Changi.

We were not much worse for our experience and had learned something about the mentality of our captors.

Life in Changi returned to its normal monotony, relieved a little by a change of quarters. We moved from the sand pit into wooden huts with concrete floors. It was a much more habitable and cleaner place. No sand here to get into our food and clothes. We had been squatting anywhere available to eat our meals but now we had a small marquee to use as a dining tent and also to use in our "leisure" hours. One of my pals made a chess set from odd pieces of wood, carving them with a blade of an old pen knife. A piece of cloth with pencilled squares served as a board. Other men soon followed his example until games of chess could be seen in progress everywhere. For myself, I dreamed of chess! The game was a great boon to us all. So many men were in poor physical condition due to lack of vitamins that they could do little more than sit about all day.

Skin diseases were rife and the irritation was greatest at night.

Often I would sit for hours outside the hut, but I was very seldom alone. The first stages of beri beri became apparent, causing my legs and feet to ache the whole time. When the moon was full we would sit outside the hut and play chess by moonlight. The MO's did their best from their scanty supplies of medicaments. We had our first taste of rice polishings – rich in vitamin B but only swallowed with the greatest effort. The stuff looked like a type of bran given to animals, it tasted terrible too, but I did manage to swallow and keep down the couple of spoonfuls a day being issued at the time. The food didn't help much either, meals were getting far worse. Rice was still our staple diet accompanied by "Air Raid" stew, so called for the obvious reason that the water in which the odd potato top floated, was all clear.

At this time much of the rice being issued was "limed". I never did discover why or how, but it was yellow in appearance and in spite of all efforts in washing the stuff before cooking, the end result, as far as we were concerned, was barely edible. We were always hungry.

Lice added to our misery. I recalled the conversation I had heard between my father and other "old sweats" about the best way of dealing with the pests. Running a burning faggot along the seams was one of their methods we tried. We also boiled our clothes and hunted for them singly to squash them between our thumb nails. Any method that killed them was good enough for us. And so the days dragged by – poor meals, lice, bugs and disease, only relieved by chess and rumour. To us a rumour was a "bore hole" referring to the place from whence it originated. The sanitary arrangements at Changi, although primitive and crude, were excellent compared to the almost non-existent ones which we were to experience later in Thailand, those of us who went to work on the railway. The Changi bore hole, was as its name implies, a hole, perhaps a foot in diameter, bored to a depth of anything from twelve to sixteen feet. Boxes resembling commodes, without a base, were placed on top, there could be up to a dozen of these seats placed side by side. By necessity men had to spend a great deal of their time on these bore holes, and it was during these sessions that stories were invented, swopped and enlarged upon.

A real place for congregating to hear the latest news was "Rumour Hill", a piece of high ground on which remained the bottom half of what must have been a huge tree, for it was broken off about sixty feet from the ground. In the evening men would gather here and swop rumours. After greeting a mate from another unit the next logical step to the conversation would be "have you heard the latest bore hole?".

"They say that there is a fleet off Singapore and we are to be taken away to a neutral Country."

"The Argentine, I heard."

"Good. We should get beef for a change."

"It's more likely we're going to be exchanged for Japanese Internees in America and Britain."

"They say that men's suits in England are being made without lapels and pockets to save cloth."

"Women's skirts are six inches above the knee."

"Blimey and the Americans are about too!"

But the rumour about Red Cross ships in Singapore turned out to have more foundation than the story that we were all to be tattooed with the rising sun on our foreheads and sent to the Argentine.

One evening a dozen or more lorries loaded with boxes bearing Red Cross markings drove past our area into the camp. These were followed by more the next day. Men strained their necks and nearly became contorted in efforts to read the labels on the boxes as they passed. The things some men saw on the labels were beyond belief. But here was something better than a rumour this time.

After the Red Cross supplies had been checked and listed they were presumably distributed equally among various sections of the camp. The South African Red Cross was responsible for sending what we received and their gifts included corned beef, tins of meat and vegetables, fish, cheese and fruit. There was also sugar and other stores in bulk. Each of us in the Cambridgeshires received a tin of milk, some biscuits and sixty Victory cigarettes.

I started smoking again. Our meals immediately improved one hundred per cent, the "air raid" stew became far more tasty, had more substance and we even had tea with sugar, and a drink of real cocoa at night. But not everyone was satisfied. Were the supplies being issued in sufficient quantities to make up for the vitamin deficiencies from which we suffered? In some other units the supplies had been issued equally, direct to the men, and not to the cook house, this was what most of us thought should have happened to ours. Supposing some of us were sent to other camps, what would happen to our share of the food intended for us? We didn't like the idea of all the stuff being hoarded in control of a few. Many of us were suspicious as to what exactly was happening to the bulk of our rations in any case; the officers and senior NCO's were feeding separately, was their diet exactly the same as ours? We never saw them eat it, they were not sharing our accommodation.

But the officer in charge was adamant and all the men got out of their moan was the unwanted right to say "I told you so" later.

With the food came a supply of clothing which included good leather boots and hats after the pattern of the English trilby. There were only a few to go round but being without reasonable footwear I received a pair of boots. Our officers seemed to think we were becoming too slack and some attempt was made to tighten up discipline. An order was issued for the benefit of all those lucky enough to receive a hat. "Hats will be worn with a dent down the centre. They will not be worn on the side of the head. The practice of writing names on the hats is to cease forthwith."

We had now been POW's for the best part of eight months and we in the Cambridgeshires had been getting far more than our share of discipline, as far as the ordinary soldier was concerned. I for one was becoming quite bolshy. Whose prisoners were we anyway? Things were unpleasant enough without being chased around by our own officers and senior NCO's from morning till night. It all seemed so petty, men belonging to other units, sited elsewhere in Changi, didn't appear to be having the same problem.

I must say that I was not against all attempts at discipline, however. We were experiencing an unpleasant period of petty thieving. Although most of us had next to nothing in the way of kit and clothing, there were a very few men always ready to steal a blanket from a dying comrade. In an attempt to prevent and stamp out this practice in our camp area, a number of night patrols were organised. Unfortunately a very small minority of men persisted in this low form of habitual thieving throughout our POW's days – I suppose they were immune from any pangs of conscience.,

It was absolutely necessary and vital for men under these conditions to keep as clean as circumstances would allow, and maintain a high standard of hygiene both personal and where communal arrangements were concerned. I concede that if strict supervision had not been maintained in this area some weaker characters could easily have adopted a "don't care, what's the use" attitude and made conditions worse for all of us.

Did one of our senior officers, sitting on his backside in the shade, think we would soon be free to fight again? Perhaps he, or they, thought the Allies were about to launch an offensive to release us. We certainly hadn't heard this one on the bore hole! Perhaps it was an attempt to prevent boredom. Whatever the reason, training courses were arranged for NCO's out of sight of enemy eyes in the coconut grove. It was all rather stupid and pointless as the majority of men were too emaciated to be able to do any exercises.

We were also instructed to make secret weapons for personal use, I remember a Sergeant Major being very proud of a sword stick he had managed to assemble by using a piece of iron in hollow bamboo. Some had even made bows and arrows.

Men were returning daily from the working parties for hospital treatment and the huts were becoming overcrowded again. My pal came back from River Valley with slight beri beri in his legs, he was glad to return, although it meant leaving the last member of our Royston trio in sole charge of the Imperial Palace. The death rate was lower than it had been, but there were still several burials a week in the cemetery a hundred yards from our camp.

Then another rumour came true. A large party of men were wanted to go somewhere north of Singapore to build a railway. Only fit men were to go. We in the Cambridgeshires paraded and the MO selected the fittest men. Such a large number was required that we nearly all found ourselves in the party classified as fit. In any case my pal and I were. I wasn't sorry to be selected. I thought a change of air might help our ailments, at least the time should pass more quickly, but what about the Red Cross parcels now? Each of us received nine tins of food, however, and strict instructions not to eat them until ordered. With Selarang fresh in our minds we saw the wisdom of this. The remainder of the Red Cross was to be left behind for those not travelling to the railway. We were told we would be separated from our officers and probably be mixed up with other units but we must remember we belonged to the Cambridgeshires. We weren't given much time to prepare but as we were ordered to travel as light as possible, our preparations mainly consisted of separating our few possessions from the home-made comforts we had managed to build for ourselves in Changi. All I had was socks, shirt, shorts, a patched blanket, mess tin, spoon and water bottle, tied up in an old tatty groundsheet. Not much I could leave behind.

I visited pals in other units and the hospital, and said my farewells, hoping to meet them again back in England. I had a look round the graves in the cemetery, by this time there were several hundred men buried there, a number from my own regiment.

We were given a concert the night before we left and thoroughly enjoyed it, especially one turn given by three of our chaps dressed up as Hitler, Mussolini and Tojo, while look-outs were posted in case any Nip came along. There was no interruption, however, and sitting there watching the show it felt like a farewell concert before embarkation.

Chapter 9

Train to Thailand

"I have never managed to lose my old conviction that travel narrows the mind."
G. J. Chesterton

Early next morning we moved to a nearby square where we were formed into parties of twenty-five to await trucks and guards to take us to Singapore Railway Station. Without too much delay, which made a change, we were on the trucks and away. We had a surprise on reaching the station about two hours later, at least those of us who had worked at River Valley. There was Dysentery Dick, Bull Frog and several of our old guards, smiling and generous, offering cigarettes and coffee to prisoners they recognised. Much as I hated the Nips these men from River Valley were the best I had met. They had some regard for human life.

We were put into covered steel trucks, about twelve feet long and six feet wide, thirty to thirty-five men in each. Those of us who had skin diseases were put together, to prevent others being infected. In my truck there were thirty three of us with our bundles of kit, and all we could do was to sit in a cramped position, or perhaps stand up. There was no room to stretch or lie down. After being told that we would be travelling several days and nights like this, and that we would not be allowed to leave the truck without Nip orders, we moved off. Conditions in our truck were extremely uncomfortable, it should be said unbearable. The sun beat down on the steel sides and roof, during the day the heat was appalling. The sides became too hot to touch, while at night they were bitterly cold. Sleep was out of the question. When it rained, the side sliding door would only partially shut, and in no time water poured in, swamping the floor, saturating us and our kits.

D. SKIPPEN 1987

Photograph of the exterior of a steel wagon, similar to the ones used to transport POW's to Thailand.

To add to our general discomfort all the men in our wagon were suffering from various forms of skin disease, we were sweaty, unwashed and unshaven, bleary-eyed and filthy. It was a nightmare journey and lasted four days and nights during which time we were jolted, bounced and crashed about like so many sacks of potatoes. The railway line was a single track and at times we were halted in a siding to allow other trains to pass. We stopped twice a day for hasty meals, of rice and messy stew. Only the meal orderlies were allowed to alight, and they had to be exceptionally quick, the slower ones received clouts from the guards. By the track was an accumulation of filth, excreta and millions of flies. It showed that other travellers had used the stop for the same purpose as ourselves. Calls of nature were also relieved by hanging one's backside out of the wagon, supported by pals, as the train clattered on. To urinate was a little less hazardous operation except for one of our number who was jammed in the corner. His need to relieve himself occurred more often than most. To make matters worse he was afflicted with a very bad stammer. "I mmm must ggg go" he'd

POW's in a steel railway wagon on their way to Thailand.

CHARLES THRALE

stutter and would commence to struggle the seven or eight feet to the open door of the wagon. Poor old Sid. With kit, arms, legs and cramped up bodies all over the place, indiscriminately treading on all and sundry, and having to endure all manner of abuse, good natured and otherwise, it would take him twenty minutes to reach the point of relief; then alas it would be in vain. He would have to clamber back, causing the same disturbance, to try again later.

One of the lads, who professed to have had vast experience with horses, suggested that Sid's problems could be solved if, when he was making an attempt, we all in unison made a continuous whistling sound, like running water. We did, but it didn't do any good for Sid. Perhaps it was just as well we had little or no water to drink.

The countryside varied from flat land, rubber plantations, paddy fields and jungle. I suppose much of it could have been called beautiful by those of us able to see it, had we been in different circumstances.

Eventually we came to the Thailand border where we halted for quite a long time. It was here we were told that our destination was somewhere near Bangkok the capital. We were warned by the Nips that the Country was full of thieves, and that whenever the train stopped we would be besieged by natives who would even steal the hats from our heads if we leaned out of the trucks. We didn't believe this but found out later it was quite true. Whenever the train stopped, Thai natives swarmed everywhere, offering money and cigarettes in exchange for old fountain pens, watches and cigarette cases. No matter how often the guards chased them off they gathered round again and several men did lose their hats.

On first impression any racial difference between the Malays and Thais was not immediately apparent. They were a tough looking lot, having a broader physique than Malays and perhaps lighter in colour, rather more like the Chinese. Most of the men wore scarves round their waists and over their shorts, turned down into a sort of bow which hung down in front of them. I was impressed by the snow white shirts which the better class were wearing. We also saw the odd Thai soldier in light brown uniform, they looked more like bus conductors to me. At one stop I saw several Buddhist priests in their saffron robes and sandals. They all looked young and intelligent, very clean and all smiles under their shaven heads.

Continuing on for what seemed an age, passing through countryside mainly paddy and jungle, we arrived at another station. We were told that this was Ban Pong and the end of our journey, we could all get out and stretch our stiff and cramped limbs. A fresh lot of guards took over. Then, filthy and weary we formed up outside the station to be counted. The Nips were most anxious not to have lost any of us, and after endless counts, much shouting and excited argument they were satisfied we were all present. Our camp was situated a couple of miles away, we were to march there with our kit. Anything must be an improvement on the last four days and nights!

Ban Pong was a small town, about thirty kilometres from Bangkok. It had fairly good roads and many native shops, wooden fronted, on either side of the main street. With its wooden buildings it looked to me like one of the Western cities in cowboy films, except that it was far more shabby and scruffy. The local population appeared very interested, and lined the streets to watch us move off. Leaving the centre of the town the area deteriorated, filthy looking pigs and mangy dogs rooted beside the road amidst mud and all kinds of refuse.

Our camp was on the other side of Ban Pong from the station and what a shock we had when we saw it. Composed of tumble down huts and fenced in by bamboo, the entire area was under black stinking mud and water. The huts were about eighty yards long having an inverted "V" shaped roof supported on flimsy bamboo poles, sloping down each side to about two feet from the ground. These roofs were thatched with atap but there were no sides as such to the huts. In the hut we entered were two long platforms two feet off the ground with a central gangway about six feet wide between them. We ploughed through filthy water, mainly raw sewage, more than twelve inches deep, to reach the entrance. Before we could enter, the body of a POW was taken out! The poor devil had died that morning.

This was a fine welcome! The platform at one end was completely submerged and the whole hut flooded with mucky water. In it were tins, banana skins, excreta and all manner of disgusting filth. We cleaned up as best we could and settled down to get the rest we so badly needed. Ban Pong camp at the time we were there was a squalid uninhabitable mess. Most of the huts were in a similar state to ours. The whole ground surface was covered in several inches of black slimy mud. The place swarming in mosquitoes and flies. Latrines consisted of bamboo platforms covering deep trenches with small openings over which men squatted side by side, there were no partitions or protective screens. Thousands of "blue-bottles" swarmed round the area while millions of white maggots occupied the surrounding ground. The approach to this disgusting place was through yet another sea of mud.

Reluctantly we handed over the tins of Red Cross issue we had carried from Changi, these having been brought to supplement the anticipated poor rations. Quite a number of us were far from happy to do so. Men from other units had already eaten their issue at Singapore, now because we were no longer a complete group of Cambridgeshires, but were being combined with other units, we would be sharing our issue with them. However, I am certain that those in charge of the Cambridgeshires had acted wisely, and in the best interest of the majority by their action, in spite of my also being convinced that a very small minority, in positions of privilege, did well out of the arrangement.

Water was obtained from a well some hundreds of yards away. Not the sort of well normally seen in parts of rural England. No ropes used here. A long bamboo pole was lowered down the well, this in turn was hinged at the top to another pole weighted at the opposite end and fixed to a hinged contraption several yards from the centre of the well. Buckets attached to the bamboo pole were lowered and raised by a counter-balanced, see-saw motion. A big problem was the lack of containers in which to carry the precious commodity back to camp. Several had already been lost down the well, as we were far from being expert at this native art. One of our party, "Snowy", the Sergeant I mentioned earlier, earned the gratitude of local camp prisoners and we watched him in amazement as he slid naked into the well again and again, retrieving nearly twenty lost containers in the space of as many minutes.

While in Ban Pong we met several Cambridgeshires who had left Changi a short time before us. They told us unbelievable stories about the railway, the jungle where we were destined to go, of Nip brutality and POW deaths. Our prospects didn't seem too rosy. What a paradise Changi had been compared to this. Surely nowhere could be worse than this place.

On the brighter side we were able to eat our fill of bananas. It was possible to buy fifteen to twenty for ten cents from the Thai women traders who sneaked up to the camp fence in spite of Nip attempts to drive them away. Two of these vendors were caught whilst we were there, and the Nips tied them to a tree for several hours before releasing them to do the same again later.

One good feature about the place was a swim in the river, no costumes of course, but who cared, it gave us an illusion of freedom. It was a relief to learn that our stay in Ban Pong would be brief, two days in fact, sufficient time to give us a foretaste of what was to come.

At noon on the third day we were on the move again, where to

'Pom pom' boat. A common sight on the rivers and similar to the ones used to convey POW's and supplies over the River Kwai Noi, before the bridges were built, and indeed after they had been destroyed by Allied bombing.

we didn't know, I don't think many of us cared, anywhere must surely be better than splashing about in the raw sewage of Ban Pong. Packed in lorries, an improvement on the steel sided trucks, we travelled approximately thirty-five kilometres until reaching another camp built on similar lines to the one we had left, but not quite so derelict. It was sited on a large flat open space which we learned later had been used as an airfield by the Nips attacking Malaya. The camp was on the outskirts of a town called Kanchanburi. We were given the usual meal of rice and weak vegetable stew and told that this was another temporary stop, the following day we would continue the journey on foot.

During the night it rained and it was still teeming down when we marched off in the morning. We went through the town until arriving at a green opposite the local gaol. Here we were split into small parties and taken to the banks of a muddy river. Barges awaited us, and once we had boarded, we were towed across the river in small parties by a primitive looking motor boat. Disembarking the other side we had now finished with any built up area of civilization. Here onwards it was jungle, jungle and still more jungle, with small areas of paddy here and there. Slipping and staggering in single file along the muddy track, we trudged in the pouring rain for three or four kilometres until coming to a clearing where several bamboo huts had been built. We were glad to get out of the rain into the hut designated. It was built of bamboo and atap like all the other huts in the Thailand camps.

The sleeping platforms were higher from the ground than any

we had yet seen and were made of split bamboo, flattened out to look like planks, wonderful places for bugs to hide until feeding time! No nails or hammers used here. All the bamboo poles were tied together with strips of slithered bark from another type of tree, these strips or ties as we came to know them, having been previously soaked in water to make them pliable. The roofs were thatched with atap, leaves stripped from palms, individual pieces all faced the same way, bent over and sewn onto a three feet lath of bamboo by the use of even thinner slivers of bamboo. A well-thatched roof would be pretty well rain-proof, one that was skimped, and many were, would leak like a sieve.

So this was Chungkai camp. Besides huts for the POW's there were also huts for the Nips; better built and more roomier than ours. The Nip guardroom, Headquarters and a canteen made up the heart of the camp, surrounded by six colossal trees, providing shade from the fiercest sun. The canteen had three sections, Imperial Japanese Army, British Officers and British Other Ranks. It was administered by three Thais and two Chinese. Open only a few hours a day it closed at nine in the evening. The snacks obtainable looked and smelt delicious, however, to the average prisoner like me that was about all we could do, look and smell, one snack cost the equivalent of half a week's pay and a packet of cigarettes about the same. Officers had not been working up until this time, but they were receiving substantially more pay than the ordinary soldier. I never did know how much, but it certainly enabled them to purchase the little extra food or comfort, to make their primitive existence more tolerable. There was supposed to be an arrangement, whereby the Nips advanced this money, and the recipients agreed to repay it when the war was over.

Chungkai was to become our working base for the immediate future, from now on we would be known as Number Two Company, Number Two Working Battalion and were warned to be ready for work on the railway the following day.

Chapter 10

Chungkai

"Slavery is no scholar, no improver; it does not love the whistle of the railroad."

Emerson

We were up before dawn the next morning to receive our breakfast of rice and jungle stew, we wouldn't have known the difference had it only been warm water, it was usually too dark to see what we ate. It was just getting light after our scrambled meal, when we were paraded by our huts to await the arrival of our guards. They were Koreans this time, in fact from here on most of our guards were Koreans. I found them very similar in appearance to the Japanese. They were probably slightly bigger and perhaps a little better looking than the guards we had encountered up to now. Their uniforms were almost identical to the Nips except for badges of rank. The Nips had three classes of privates and were distinguished by the number of yellow stars fastened to a strip of red cloth worn on the left breast. NCO's wore bars and stars of various sizes and colours whereas most officers had silver bars and invariably wore riding boots.

There were no NCO's or officers among the Koreans, they all wore a red five-pointed star on their left sleeve. Koreans usually carried out the main guard duties while the Nips were actually in charge of the railway work. It was nothing to find a Private or Lance Corporal in charge of a POW camp containing a number of guards and several hundred prisoners. We discovered to our cost, as time went on, that even the lowest ranking private appeared to have licence to hand out bashings whenever he felt the inclination to do so. Koreans or Nips they all became the same to us, we always referred to them as "Nips" except when we found other less complimentary names to use. They had a peculiar method of summoning a prisoner to them, calling "Kurra", they would extend a hand toward the victim, palm downwards, and flap it up and down from the wrist.

We were marched through the jungle to another clearing about thirty yards wide and stretching as far as we could see in both directions. This was the area that had been prepared by other POWs to take the railroad track. Halted by a large hut we found it to be a tool shed. Here were more Nips standing beside rows of tools laid out in groups of five. There were shovels, picks and chunkals, this was a native tool, it had a large spade-like blade fitted at right angles to a wooden shaft three or four feet long. In addition there were sacks, bamboo poles and baskets. By grunts and signs it was conveyed to us that we were to pick up these tools and follow the guards.

We did so and walked about half a kilometre, passing parties of men already on the job. We soon saw what we had to do. At every twenty yards or so, profiles had been set up to mark where the railway embankment was to be made. These profiles were made from thin bamboo cane, three were placed vertically in the ground with a long one horizontally along the top and others sloping down from either side at an angle outwards to the ground. It was all very crude but this was to be the shape of the completed embankment. The profiles naturally varied in size according to the level and height of the ground surface, they were anything from three to twenty feet high, but in fact perhaps six feet on average.

Parties were allocated sections of the cleared jungle. Our party was shown a strip about fifty yards long and told to get busy. The earth had to be dug from either side of the cleared jungle, taken and dumped between the profiles. We were split into smaller groups of five or six men, some dug, picked and loaded the soil into baskets, the baskets looked like coal scuttles and had a handle at each side, others humped them and emptied their contents between the profiles. Stretchers were made by using the sacks and poles. A two man job this, but whatever part one played in the chain, the work ground laboriously on, dig, fill, carry, dump and spread. I often wondered if the slaves looked like this building Egyptian pyramids thousands of years BC.

Throughout most of our time toiling on the railway it was necessary to work in similar small groups. We tried to form our own little gangs, varying the labour between us and as far as possible keeping up a continuous discussion on all manner of subjects to keep our spirits high

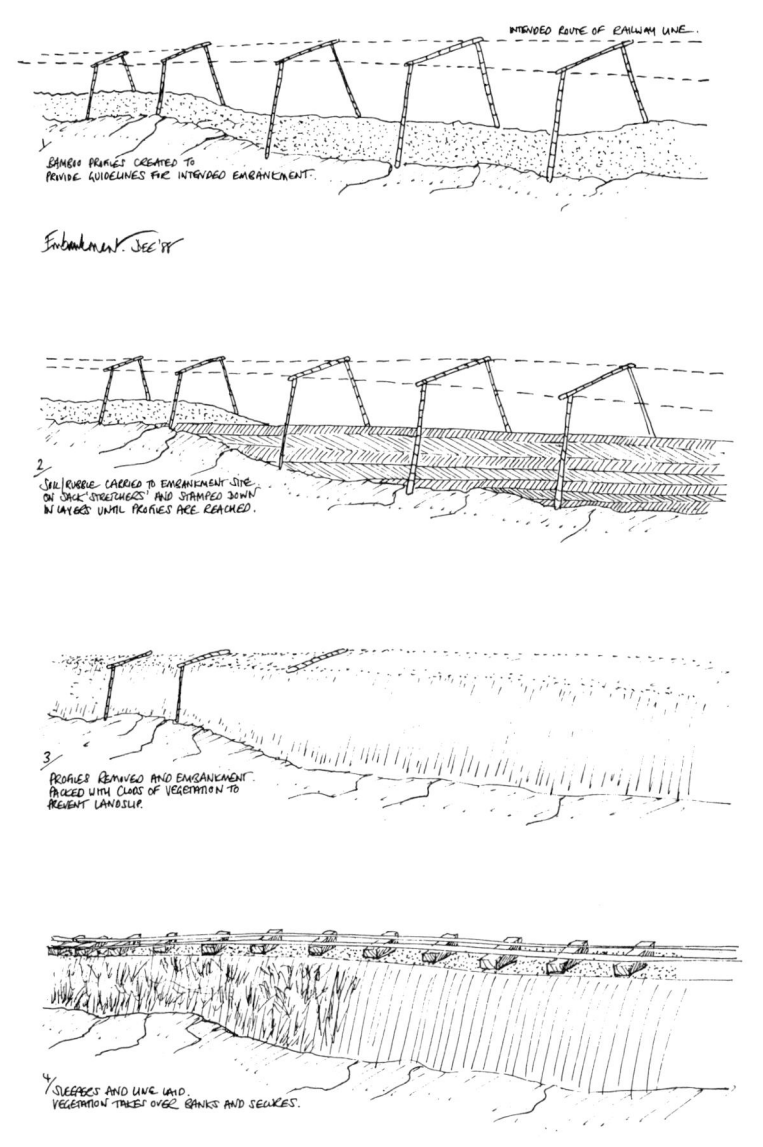

An impression of the perhaps unusual, but effective, method in which the contours of the railway embankment took shape.

We were allowed one small "Yasumi" during the morning and a little longer break at midday when we were able to down tools and eat our meal of plain boiled rice and a spoonful of sugar, our drink was a mug-full of boiled muddy water. Work then continued until eight thirty in the evening when the tools were checked, handed in at the shed and we returned to camp. A wash by the river, a meal of more plain boiled rice and jungle stew and so to bed on our bamboo slats, exhausted and soon asleep.

This was typical of our first few days on the railway, the same old routine, a meal in the dark, off to the embankment as dawn broke, dig, load, carry and dump. Back to camp at night, eat and fall asleep.

But after those first few days the rain spells increased and our situation became far worse.

It rained night and day, but made no difference to what was expected of us. We plunged through ankle deep mud as soon as it became daylight. At the embankment we found our holes of yesterday full of water and, after slogging away all day, would return to camp at night and find that place a quagmire also. We were so weary and exhausted that we always slept soundly enough, but one morning we awoke to find that the river had overflowed its banks, and we were marooned on our bed platforms. This was even worse than our experience in Ban Pong. The latrines had been flooded and most of the contents were floating in two feet of water under our beds. Boots and any other articles left near the water had been washed away.

The cookhouse was just as bad, completely flooded and, as a result, we got nothing to eat until late into the day. We gathered what belongings we could find and waded waist-deep through disgusting filth to a higher part of the camp. Here we hung about wet and stinking while our officers negotiated with the Nips, getting us excused work for the day and, we hoped, some drier accommodation.

Eventually the Nips took our party through the jungle to a Thai Kampong, a small native village, in the centre of which stood a little Thai school, built on poles about six feet from the ground. Some were able to find shelter under this building while the remainder made the best of things round the outside, seeking any cover available. The one-day off, and next morning it was a repeat of the same routine, collect tools, dig, carry and spread, with the odd clout of encouragement from the Nip guards.

Work went badly. Evening came and we looked forward to

getting back to our temporary camp and some rest. But the Nips had other ideas. Despite the rain, which had started to pour again, we were ordered to keep working. We carried on until darkness came and it was impossible to see. We must pack up now. "No one can see," we told the Nips and dropped our production rate. We thought we had been successful, but then to our dismay more Nips arrived with acetylene lamps for us to work by. We were tired, hungry and saturated. Men began throwing down their tools. The Nips dealt out blows to the offenders, made some stand for long periods holding tools or baskets of earth above their heads.

We continued working until one thirty the following morning, when we returned to our temporary camp where we sat or stood under the Thai school until dawn. The only alternative was to go outside in the mud and rain. When daylight came we went back to work, still in our wet clothes. We worked until dark and again the lamps were brought out. We were told that we were to do a certain amount of work each day and would not be allowed to knock off until it was completed. This was the pattern for several days and nights but at last we got back to our finishing time of about nine in the evening. The floods subsided and we were able to return to our old quarters.

We had seen a Nip officer a number of times as we worked and now discovered that he was the cause of most of our troubles. The work on our section of the railway was under his direction. His name was Taramoto and he was a swine. A shade taller than the average Nip, he wore horn-rimmed glasses, pith helmet, and long slacks tucked into his riding boots. He never tired of telling us that he hated the English – as if we hadn't guessed that for ourselves! Rumour had it that he had been slighted by Englishmen before the war and was doing his best to work off his grudge on us. It certainly seemed like it. He introduced a system of task work whereby the embankment was divided into sections. These sections were allocated to groups of fifty men who had to move so many cubic metres of earth every ten days. If we finished the allotted task within the ten day period, the remainder of the time would be allowed for "Yasumi".

How we worked to get done in time and get that few hours Yasumi on the tenth day! But only once! We found that if we finished early Taramoto would make sure that the task was substantially increased for the next ten days. In future we arranged our work so that it was more or less completed on the tenth day without it being necessary for lights to be brought out. We also devised ways of reducing our work rate, without making it obvious to the Nips. Should at any time the vigilance of the guards waver, or be distracted, we would dump large logs or roots into the embankment hastily covering them with earth. It gave us some feeling of satisfaction, perhaps we were doing a little towards sabotaging the railway, and at the same time using less effort to complete our allotted task. Taramoto had no monopoly of craftiness. Little did we think that the time might come when we would travel on the track ourselves. As far as we were concerned we were building a very un-'permanent way'.

The loss of tools, or even the sale of them to natives, gave Taramoto his chance to punish us, and many a time after we had finished our work we were kept searching the area, looking for missing gear. One night he was so enraged at the losses that he ordered the whole party of us to stand to attention for the remainder of the night. "If mosquito come, you will not move," and so we stood for several hours, when eventually we were allowed to return to our huts.

Chungkai was run on similar lines to River Valley, except that our work never varied. Always that blasted railway. A Nip Colonel Yanagida was in charge of the camp, he had an interpreter named Adachi, referred to by us as Ada, a staff of several Nip engineers and a number of Korean guards. He was a very small man, possibly no more than five feet tall and quite a character. He had a special set of PE exercises all his own, which he insisted our officers should parade us to see. We watched him without excitement, but perhaps muted amusement. His physical training seemed to involve the minimum amount of physical exertion although he claimed it would enable him to live to be a hundred. He would attend the funerals of our men and make a speech at the grave saying how sad it was for men to die so far from home.

I remember another time when, from an elevated position on the steps of his office, he advised none of us to attempt escape as it was hopeless, if caught it would mean death. He felt sure that before long we would return home to our loved ones. This last remark started rumours circulating.

Yanagida was quite a decent little chap but he appeared to have little control over the Nip engineers, Taramoto in particular.

British officers were in charge of the working parties, passing on the instructions of the Japanese technicians and guards. It was their job to see that we had our share of Yasumi's and generally watch over our interests. Back in camp the general administration of prisoners was in their hands. They were responsible for supplying the working parties, distributing the rations made available to us, and presumably appointing fellow prisoners to cook them. During the first few months on the railway this was all the officers were called upon to do. There appeared to be quite a lot of them in proportion to the number of other ranks, and only the odd one was being called upon to accompany a working party.

Their leisure time came to a dramatic end later, when, taking advantage of a temporary absence of Colonel Yanagida, Taramoto ordered all officers to parade. He told them that in future they would have to supply working parties from their midst on similar lines to the men. They objected, quoting the Geneva Convention, and at first refused to comply with his orders. However, after being given the option "work or be shot" they came to the conclusion that it was perhaps more prudent to be alive, and work, than to refuse and be dead.

Despite normal skin complaints, from which most of us seemed to be suffering, I worked continuously on the railway, doing the same repetitive job until December 20 1942, when I caught dysentery again, and was admitted to hospital. This wasn't the best way to escape the severities of Taramoto, but it was one way, and I saw little of him until I was at another camp later on. There our CO received a letter from him thanking us for the work we had done on the railway and asking us to accept a personal gift as a mark of his appreciation. The personal gift was fifty cents! Sixpence to be shared between sixty or seventy men. Taramoto was determined to work off his grudge! "I hate you English."

Chapter 11

Christmas 1942 and Dysentery

> *"One day I sat thinking, almost in despair; a hand fell on my shoulder and a voice said reassuringly; 'Cheer up, things could be worse'. So I cheered up and, sure enough, things got worse."*
>
> James Hagerty

The "hospital" at Chungkai was not very large at this time, as there had not been a lot of sickness in the camp, by POW's standards, to warrant a larger one. Up to the time of our arrival only one man had died here, but now never a day went by without a death. Thirty men had been buried in two or three weeks. The huts were similar to those in which we lived but much smaller and there were separate ones for dysentery, malaria, skin diseases, surgical and medical cases.

The dysentery ward accommodated thirty patients and there was only one vacant "bed" space when I was admitted, and we were packed in shoulder to shoulder. By this time paper of any sort was becoming a thing of the past, and for toilet use, non-existent. Leaves from trees were used instead. I was never completely confined to bed during this bout of dysentery, and could gather leaves from the trees outside the hut, both for myself and for chaps who were too weak to get up. Being prepared was everything. A pause to gather leaves on the dash to the latrine might, and often did, have disastrous results.

I started my treatment on a fluid diet, a little clear liquid which may have experienced the hint of green vegetable in the making. Within two days I was put on the light diet and developed an appetite that would have made the "full" look silly. But even so I couldn't get through the day without a dozen dashes to the latrine and almost as many at night.

I think it was on December 23 1942 we were given our second card to send home. This time it was already printed and we had the option of several phases:
"I am well."
"I am in hospital."
"I am working for pay."
"I have received Red Cross parcels."
"From .... ,"
Nearly all of us sent the message "I am well" although some were nearly dead, in fact the chap occupying the space next to me did send this message and two days later was buried in Chungkai cemetery after sending these comforting words to his family. I doubt that they received the card until the war was over.

On Christmas morning I awoke to the sound of Carols being sung in the small atap Church near the ward, and later on the Padre came in and wished us all as happy a Christmas as possible under the circumstances. He held a brief, quiet service before leaving. My thoughts were far away, both in time and locality. I wondered how the loved ones were at home. Perhaps they didn't know if I was alive or dead, I had no idea how they were. They certainly would have been unable to imagine our conditions had I sent a card phrased "I am in hospital". No beds, bedding or even toilet paper here. Still there were many chaps worse off than me this first Christmas, many were dead, and many more wouldn't live to see another.

Being on light diet over Christmas I was prevented from having any of the little extra that had been scrounged for the festive season. I could manage the few cigarettes brought to me but had to forego the peanuts. Shortly after breakfast I heard from a pal what was happening in other parts of the camp. The Nips had granted a day's rest for Christmas, and all the lads had contributed something from their pay to purchase several little extras, including a cow for seventeen dollars. It was not much bigger than a greyhound and not much fatter.

While sick we received no pay, workers were being paid one dollar every ten days, the equivalent to a penny a day. In the afternoon several members of an impromptu concert party gave a few turns in the wards before the main camp concert in the evening. I heard later that it was a great success, one item in particular being tumultuously received – the appearance of the "Jungle Princess" – one of the chaps dressed up as a girl. The programme also included a catchy song based on the latest bore hole rumour. It was called the "Chungkai Blues" and contained a prophetic line "Ships will meet us at Rangoon". They did – three years later!

> "I've lost those Chungkai blues
> Just heard the latest bore hole news
> War is going to end this new year
> It's not going to be a blue year
> We will take the railroad track
> As the shortest journey back.
> So pack your kits and say Goodbye
> Roll on the boat, Oh me! Oh my!
> I've lost those Chungkai Blues.
> Ships will meet us at Rangoon
> We will see Southampton soon
> We will have a Scotch and soda
> At the Pass of Three Pagoda.
> Goodbye to Chungkai, Chungkai
> C – H – U – N – G – K – A – I
> Chungkai blues."

While I was in the dysentery ward the first Allied planes came over. In bright moonlight they followed the course of the river and we heard them return two hours later. We were told afterwards there had been a heavy raid on Bangkok. Months passed before we heard our planes again but these first few were regarded as the harbingers of freedom.

We were experiencing a similar sort of climate as a mild winter in Britain, at least as far as the nights were concerned. During the day it was very hot, but when evening came the temperature dropped dramatically, and we shivered under our scanty covering, finding sleep almost impossible. The hours of daylight were passed by Bridge playing among the "up patients". The cards were battered, worn and dirty, limp through months of use but they served their purpose. Bridge playing was replaced by Monopoly later on. One of the patients had contrived to make a set.

By January 12 1943 my dysentery was much better. Adorning a suitable leaf, my daily stool specimen had been handed in for examination, a microscope still being available in this camp. I received a visit from Captain Hendry, the MO. He thought I was fit enough to return to my unit, and when I objected that I still had acute diarrhoea, opined that it would be a long time before any of us did one "twice round the pan again". "Chew every grain of rice thoroughly," he said, "and when you've done that, chew it again." I have never forgotten the advice. The MO's words of wisdom still ringing in my ears, much thinner, and decidedly weak I returned to my old bed space in the hut. The diarrhoea continued and I was put on light duties about the camp for seven days. At least I was still alive, by this time several men from our Regiment had died in Chungkai, including a Sergeant, the victim of diphtheria and malaria.

The railway was being built to run from Thailand to Burma following the line of the river Kwai Noi, at times within a few metres of its bank. POW camps had been sited at intervals and men worked in both directions, linking up the railway, some building up the embankment, in other areas making cuttings, blasting through rock or building bridges over small ravines or culverts.

About the end of January we heard that a number of men were required to go further up country on bridge building work. Sure enough our working battalion was selected, at least the so-called fit were, and although still in a weak state, I found myself included in their number.

We paraded with our kit and collection of the working party's stores, the latter included cooking utensils, food and sacks of rice. Some of the heavy gear would be going by barge and the rest man-handled by us. To add to our burden we were to carry the gear of the Nips accompanying us and the tools needed for our new type of work.

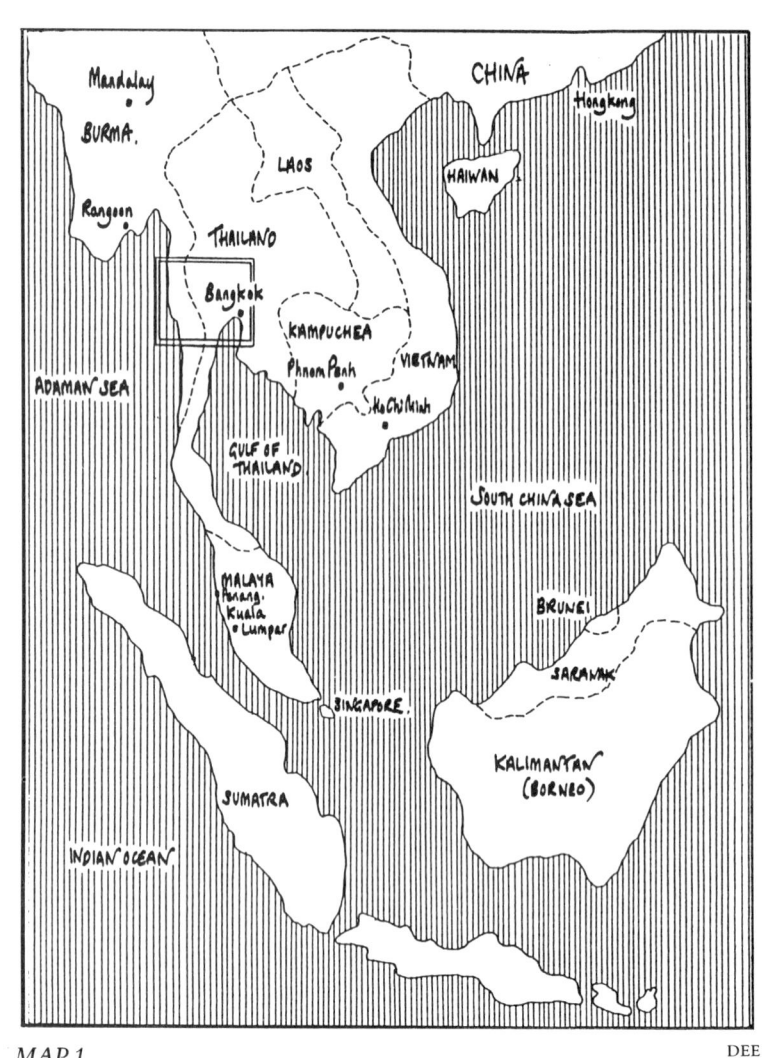

MAP 1
Map showing the general area of operations from Singapore to Burma.

Christmas 1942 and Dysentery

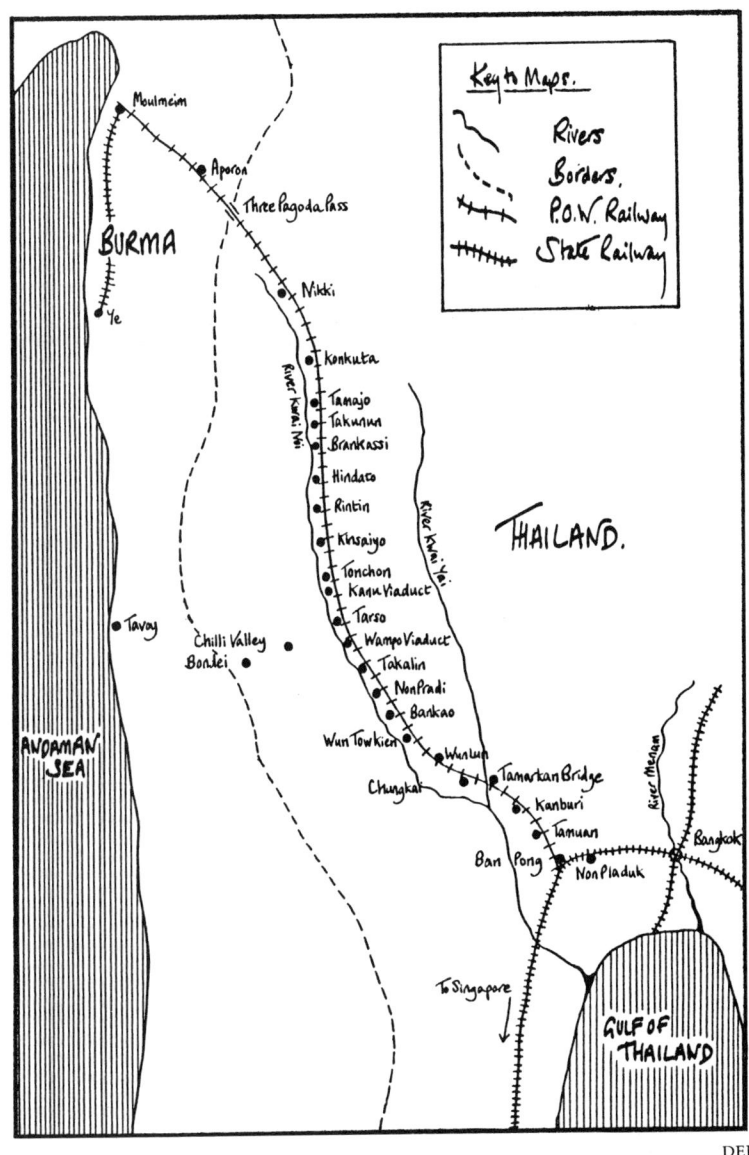

MAP 2
Enlargement of boxed area of previous map, showing route of Prisoners of War-built railway and rough positions of work-camps. Definitely not to scale.

Chapter 12

Bridge Building

"Britons never, never, never, shall be slaves."
Rule Britannia

Leaving Chungkai, we marched along the track that was to become the railway and once we had scrambled over the rocks of Chungkai quarry, where other POW's were drilling and blasting, our route continued over fairly flat country, heading, we were told, towards Wun Lun. Four hours tramping under the boiling sun made extremely thirsty going, especially when there was no water to drink, but the Nips didn't hurry us unduly and allowed us two short breaks on the way. Many men, like me, were suffering from chronic diarrhoea, and frequent unofficial individual stops were made as it became necessary for us to dash to relieve ourselves at the side of the track.

After trudging through paddy fields and belts of thick bamboo jungle we passed POW's who were working from Wun Lun and once we were through a tobacco plantation the camp itself was in view. It had been built on the edge of the railway embankment, close to the river and unlike Chungkai, which was surrounded by thick jungle, was in open country with tobacco plantations and cultivated land surrounding it.

After spending one night at Wun Lun we were on the march again next morning, heading for Wan Tai Kin, and were very weary when we eventually reached there in the late afternoon. It was a small camp built beside the river with the clearing for the railway about a kilometre distant. On arrival we had no work to do for the Nips, and after a wash in the river it wasn't long before we were asleep on the bamboo platforms in our huts.

The following morning we paraded for work. Different tools

were issued this time, cross cut saws, small hands saws of Nip design, made to be pulled instead of pushed, ropes, axes and crowbars.

Marching out of the camp we came through the clearing to a depression in the land running through the railway trace at right angles. Here our new work was explained to us. In small parties we were taken into the jungle where the Nips selected the trees they wanted us to hew down. After being felled and cut to suitable lengths they had to be carried to the dip in the track. Elephants would have jibbed at the weights we were expected to carry, but by placing poles under the trees at intervals of three feet or so, with a man on each end of the poles, we were able to struggle along slowly. Elephants were used in one or two areas but no doubt we were a cheaper form of labour and more expendable. Enormous trees were carried quite long distances through the jungle by this method, and the Nips helped us along by a smack on the face, a kick on the shins, or a bamboo across the back whenever we stumbled.

Several days of this slavery produced a pile of trees which we then proceeded to strip of bark, and saw into logs of various lengths. Each of these logs was then sharpened to a point at one end, and a hole drilled in the centre of the other, about two inches in diameter and three inches deep. Round the blunt end of the logs several strands of wire were wound, about two inches from the top. These were the piles that were to form the uprights for the bridge.

The next job was the piledriver. No mechanical artifice here. More improvisation. We made our own piledriver on the spot! Thinner trees and bamboos were cut from the jungle. With these we made a frame perhaps twenty or thirty feet high. The base about fifteen by ten feet, tapering to about one foot to two at the top, all lashed together with rope. After fixing pulleys at the top of the frame, we pulled the weight and bar into position. The former weighed several hundredweight and had a bar weighing about another hundredweight through its centre.

A pile was put into position, two men sat straddling the platform at the top, one end of the bar was sited into the hole in the pile and the other end of this centre pole tied to the top of the framework and steadied by the two men precariously sitting on top. Ropes were attached to a ring on the top of the pear-shaped weight, and from these, others led through the pulleys and outward on either side of the frame.

Bridge Building

This is an attempt to illustrate how the smaller bridges were built over culverts and depressions in the land. Similar methods, but on a much larger scale, were employed to build the big constructions over the Kwai Noi and the viaducts farther up into the jungle.

Bridge Building

The rest was simple but cruel work. Ten or so men on either side of the frame pulled the weight up and as we slackened in unison down came the weight with a thump. At first our rhythm left a lot to be desired, we often deliberately appeared not to understand exactly what was required of us, this applied on most other jobs too, the tactics held up progress but produced many beatings. The Nips ordered us to sing as we pulled, by doing this we would all keep in time. It should have been pull, one, two, three – drop, or for the Nip's benefit "Ichi Ni Asio" drop. We had many various jingles such as "Get the bastard higher" – drop. "Won't go any higher" – drop. "You're a bloody liar" – drop. "Tojo's a bastard" – drop, and many more. The Nips didn't worry too much what we sang as long as that damned weight continued to keep going up and down. Piles were driven in as far as they would go, and then the tops sawn off level to make a foundation for the bridge. Sections were cut out for joints, other trees stripped of bark, squared off then fitted across the piles. Further odd pieces were fitted here and there and the whole construction held together by iron dogs. This bridge, about twenty feet in length, took a hundred of us rather more than a week to complete.

In the course of this operation nearly every man received blows from the Nips who displayed the most unreasonable anger because we could not understand their every screamed instruction. Many a time we genuinely misunderstood an order shouted in Japanese. The result would be a Nip with a frayed temper and a prisoner with a very sore face.

Taramoto visited us on several occasions and whenever he appeared the Nips worked us harder than ever. Their fear of him, and our dislike, were about equal. Our normal working hours were from dawn to dusk. We had our usual breakfast of rice and a spoonful of sugar, this was consumed in the dark, as was the evening meal on our return to camp. Tiffin, as we came to know it by, was taken during a short break beside the job. Drink was the usual boiled muddy water from the river. During the day the heat of the sun was terrific but it was desperately cold at night, we kept fires burning outside the huts, and crowded round them most of the night but it didn't prevent us continually shivering. I didn't even have a blanket for cover at the time.

During a Yasumi in our bridge building I saw my first really big snake. Several of us were sitting quietly, having our drink of hot water when, hardly making a sound on the sun-scorched leaves, it slithered out of the undergrowth less than a yard from my feet.

Many a time I had chased and killed smaller ones, but this one must have been three inches in diameter and fifteen feet long. We jumped to our feet to run away but it turned from our direction. Had we been making a noise it would never have come near us, but we didn't think of that at the time. None of these snakes attack unless disturbed. Like other wild animals of the jungle they were rarely to be seen, being as frightened of us as we were of them. At another camp later we did see several gibbons and we frequently heard them chattering close by.

This bridge completed, our company, about a hundred men, left the rest of the battalion. We were going to build bridges further up the line and were to camp on our work sites. Carrying all our stores, tents, Nip's kit as well as our own, we marched several hours, stopping just short of Bankao. Six Nips accompanied us. We pitched the tents, one for the Nips and several more for ourselves in a dried-up paddy field on the edge of the jungle. Our next bridge was to be built less than a hundred yards away.

Shortly after we arrived several of us were taken to the river by the Nips who dynamited one place, and we swam out to collect the stunned or dead fish floating on the surface. We soon had a sack full and that night there were many fires where fish was being grilled. Needless to say we cooked more fish than the Nips gave us as our share! It was grand to get such tasty food and go to sleep with a full stomach for once!

During our short stay here we built two bridges in the same manner as the first, felling and carrying trees from the jungle, shaping them into piles, and driving them into position, first making the improvised piledriver from small trees.

It was still very cold at night and we slept around the fires where we could. Inside the tents were swarms of ants, nasty big red creatures with a powerful bite, smaller black ones were just as bad, they got into everything from mess tins to clothing. The buzz of mosquitoes filled the air and as far as we were concerned mosquito nets were a thing of the past. We often heard tom toms or drums, beating in the jungle, but in the daytime we never saw a single person except for an occasional Buddhist priest or a Thai with a few skinny cattle. We "knocked off" a small cow one day. It was a poor miserable specimen, but it went some way to improving a meal. Although not an everyday occurrence, I derived some feeling of comfort whenever I saw one of the young priests, in his saffron robe, shaven head and bare feet, picking his way along the railway track. It was cheering to conclude that at least they were free and still able to travel around more or less as they pleased. They would pass impassively by, apparently completely disinterested, and unaware of our plight, but I often wondered if they were as neutral as they appeared. Were they, perhaps, responsible for some of the news we received?

With these bridges completed we were marched off and set up another small camp four kilometres the other side of Bankao where we built two more. One of these involved still harder work as the piles were set in concrete bases. Shingle was used for this purpose and the Nips had a simple way of obtaining it. There was a plenteous supply in the river bed. A party of men had to wade out into the river and chain buckets of water, mud and stones to the beach. Here it was sifted, the shingle put into sacks and carried to the bridge site. It was no joke to carry a sack of stones on the bare back for eight hundred yards, but any man caught resting during this task was beaten up. But we did devise a system that allowed men to rest while others kept look-out. Work continued from dawn to dusk. Our food was brought to us from Bankao, and what hadn't spilled by the time it reached us was cold and unappetising.

About thirty of our party became too ill to work at all and nearly all were weak and should have been resting. I repaired to the jungle for "speedo benjo" at least ten times a day, and hardly ever reached a suitable spot in time.

Taramoto visited us again, this time on horse back. He wanted to know why so few men were working and where were the others. "They are very sick men and are resting in their tents", he was told. "Get all men out, I inspect them," ordered Taramoto. The MO refused and after several more demands was rewarded by a bashing from the Nip officer. Taramoto then inspected the tents himself and forced the men to turn out. Dysentery and malaria cases were made to work on the piledriver. One man suffering from beri beri had almost lost the use of his legs. Taramoto hit him with his sword and ordered him to run. He fell flat on his face at the attempt, and the next day with two others he was sent down country for rest.

I don't know what Tarmoto thought of our party but whatever his opinion, it was shortly after his visit that we found ourselves on the move again.

Chapter 13

Nom Pradai and Wun Lun

*"The rain it raineth every day
Upon the just and unjust fellow, But chiefly on the just, because
The unjust has the just's umbrella"*

Anon

This march or trek was one of the worst I experienced during my first two years as a prisoner. It was a very hot day, the sun beat down relentlessly. There was more kit and gear to carry than ever, as many men were too weak to take their share. Weak as we were, another man and I carried our load and in addition a large tent slung between us on a bamboo pole. We trudged through uncleared jungle and for the first part of the journey of seventeen kilometres the ninety of us kept fairly well together, but after two hours marching my partner at the other end of the pole and I could see nobody in front or behind. We halted several times hoping that the men in the rear would catch us up but nobody came. We followed a small track in the jungle, finding here and there small posts placed to indicate the site of the railway line. Sometimes we lost these signs altogether and had to retrace our steps to pick up the track again. In one area the jungle had been cleared by burning, but there seemed to be no way round it so we staggered on through. The heat left from the burnt-out trees and undergrowth was as fierce as the sun above. It was nearly dark when we caught up with some of the front party who had been waiting for us to appear. We were led off to our left and soon after arrived at our destination somewhat the worse for wear.

There were still a number of stragglers to come and while the rest of us pitched tents and scrambled a meal together, a Nip and several men went back into the jungle to bring them in.

Nom Pradai was a tented camp and new. Of the few men before us, prisoners from Java and Sumatra, there were Dutchmen, Javanese and Eurasians, with Dutchmen in the majority. We had seen them march up country a fortnight before. They all looked fit, fat and healthy, appeared to be carrying plenty of personal kit and wore good uniforms and that made the rags we were wearing seem worse than ever by comparison.

There was to be no let up. Work began the day after our march. Out from a clearing in the jungle at dawn, and the same weary work of bridge building except with an added variation this time, which was drilling and blasting rock. No pneumatic drills here. Split into pairs, we were supplied with metal drills and chisels of various lengths plus hammers of different weights. One man held a chisel while the other belted it until a small hole appeared in the rock. We did this, taking turns to hit and hold until we had made enough metre deep holes to satisfy the Nip. The holes would be charged with explosive, then it was stand clear and blast, shift the rubble and start all over again. Drilling and blasting from dawn to dark. Nothing but slavery.

The Nips thought too much time was being wasted walking from camp to work. They remedied this. We were moved to the bridge sites, we could then scramble straight out of our tents to work. Rudely awakened well before daylight, in the pitch darkness, there was little time to consider what might lay ahead for us during the day, in any case it was usually the same as the one just gone.

During the monsoon period, a small taste of which we were experiencing now, a typical day would be – stagger out of the tent, often still wet from the day before, and the effects of a leaky tent; slip and slide in mud and pouring rain to collect the usual breakfast from the cooks; perhaps there might be a chance to swill face and hands, in the water caught from the sides of the tent; the hurried meal, after which we stood in the rain awaiting Nip engineers to decide who worked where.

By the time daylight arrived, much work had already been done, and near naked bodies were glistening with a mixture of rain and sweat. Most men were pitifully thin, but nearly all had big unhealthy swollen "rice bellies" in addition to the assortment of general skin diseases, dermatitis, ringworm and the rest.

There might be a brief Yasumi during the morning, when we would be allowed to indulge in the luxury of a drink of "Char" in our case, unadulterated, recently boiled hot water. If lucky there would be an hour's break at midday for a meal and a well-earned rest, hopefully the rain would have eased for a short period and we could stretch out and relax our aching limbs.

Throughout the day a number of necessary individual breaks were made to "speedo benjo" at the side of the jungle, not forgetting the stream of screamed orders and accompanying blows from the Nips.

And so on until darkness came and no further work was possible. To get a wash after the day's hard labour meant a walk to the river, a kilometre away. Fagged out as we were at the end of the day, even the prospect of the wash we so badly needed was not sufficient to tempt us on a long trek to an ice cold river in pitch darkness. We mostly slept as we were, filthy dirty and unwashed. In any case soap was now almost unobtainable and it took a week's pay to secure a tablet. Cigarettes could no longer be bought, but native tobacco, very much like coconut matting in texture, could be obtained and after it had been washed and dried in the sun it was just about smokable. Sometimes we could buy cigarette papers at five cents for two packets, with eight to ten papers in each, but more often than not we had to make do with any odd scrap of paper that came our way.

It was seldom possible to cut one's nails, I continued to use the same method that I had perfected at River Valley, biting those accessible and tearing off excess toe nails the best I could, at the same time taking care not to make them ingrowing. Teeth were never cleaned, but hair tidied occasionally with a borrowed piece of comb. A man with defective vision would have further hardship added to his miserable existence should he break his spectacles, as many did. No optical facilities here, he had to manage somehow without. Broken specs were seldom completely discarded however, the owner of a single lens could find himself very much in demand, the combination of hot sun and a spectacle lens was one good method of creating fire, in the absence of a box of matches. Some men with large sets of dentures found themselves with problems too, break or lose his teeth and that was that. Still, there was very little to chew anyway, and a gummy smile was as good as a full-toothed one. Often more cheerful, in fact.

Rumours reached us that in many places the railway embankment had been completed, but the constant sight of parties marching up country gave lie to these. Sometimes we caught sight of men from our own regiments and shouted information to each other as they went through.

Work continued relentlessly despite the weak state of many of us, I had lost a lot of weight but many chaps had lost more. With our skinny bodies, various skin diseases and ragged clothes we were beginning to look a sorry sight.

Protests by our officers to the Nips brought no respite, though some did refuse to send men to work when they were ill and risked death for doing so. Unfortunately there were a few officers who did not try sufficiently hard, and were prepared to give in to Nip demands too easily, but more about this later.

One of our party died at Nom Pradai, the first death we had since leaving Changkai. Poor Sid, he was the man with the stammer and weak bladder in our railway wagon on the journey up from Singapore. Ragged by the rest, as is the lot of the big and clumsy. Never again would he stop us in the middle of a job with his humourless question, "Shall I ggg give you one of mmm my lectures?" "Go on Sid, let's have it." We'd say, when we felt it was his turn for a break.

Then the same question, without a trace of suspicion, slowly and heavily, "Shall I ggg give mmm my lecture on films, or mmm my Drum Set or ggg girls?"

Whatever the subject the lecture was never given. A clout from the Nips would send us back to work and Sid back to that private vacuity in which he lived. Because he knew of the chaffing that any complaint of his would receive from the rest of us, Sid always postponed the announcement of his misery until the last moment. Perhaps that's the reason he died when he did.

The bridge near our camp was completed and we received orders to pack all gear, we were on the move once more. This was early April 1943 and the news was good, if genuine, we were going down country for a rest. When we set off on the march to Bankao it was with the lightest hearts that prisoners could have. The trek back was a gruelling business, my diarrhoea becoming more serious and I had to make frequent stops on the way. It was night by the time we reached Bankao, I was all in and glad to flop down and rest. I knew I was far from fit but the fact was brought home to me on arrival. Joining up with the remainder of Number Two Battalion, I met friends who I'd not seen for several months, it was grand to join up with them again but their greeting, "Blimey Jack, how ill you look." didn't do much for my morale. I realised how down I must have become. I visited the latrine that night a dozen times. I was getting so that I couldn't control myself. I soiled my shorts and left them outside the hut and had to wash them before we moved off again in the morning. Were they dry? No! Put on wet they dried as I went along.

It was another hard march for many of us, some chaps were far worse than me. We were surprised to see that the railway embankment had nearly reached Bankao and was complete with sleepers and railway lines. Even more surprising, diesel lorries, with wheels adapted, were running up and down the line pulling more trucks bringing up sleepers and equipment. It looked as though we had built a railway after all.

We reached Wun Lun to find a small station and sidings had been built, this only amounted to a few loop lines and one or two small bamboo and atap buildings, not exactly Euston or Kings Cross.

We were put into a hut after being counted several times, I was too tired and thirsty to think about much, within a few minutes I slept.

Wun Lun was the rest camp and the first three days really were Yasumi. We spent the time repairing and washing our shabby threadbare clothes and doing the few odd jobs that make life more bearable. Up in the jungle we had been unable to spend the slightly increased Nip pay we had received, and with the great wealth of two or three dollars in our pockets, we were more than pleased to find a Thai Kampong on the edge of the camp.

Here the natives had erected a number of small shops, little shelters of bamboo and atap where they sat surrounded by their goods such as bananas, peanuts, as well as a few sweet and savoury cooked dishes, usually served up on banana leaves. The "sweets" were made of rice and tapioca and the "savouries" of vegetable or fish highly seasoned with curry or chilly. "Wog weed" for smoking was on sale as well as dried stink fish and a variety of fruit. The vendors usually had plenty of eggs to sell and as one approached their little stall, they would cry "cook, cook no cook" for either one hard boiled or the unadulterated article. As the price of one of these eggs was the equivalent of half a week's pay, and in any event nearly always had a pronounced flavour of fish, I very seldom indulged in such an expensive luxury. The money we possessed wouldn't buy very much, but while it lasted we could get the odd extra, such as a few peanuts, to supplement our rice diet, and at the time enjoy the feeling of comparative freedom. At least it should have been enjoyable but this "Shopping Centre" will

Author's own impression of a Thai woman carrying her portable shop. These vendors would appear, as if by magic, near the entrances to some of the larger camps.

always stick in my memory as it was there I received one of my protracted bashings from the Nips. Partly my fault, I was down at the Kampong during forbidden hours with another prisoner. He managed to make himself scarce when a native accused me of stealing a five cent biscuit from his stall. The bawling of the outraged trader attracted the attention of two Nips. When I saw them I knew it was too late to run. I waited for the inevitable.

One of the Nips, unfortunately for me, happened to be a well built, heavy man and, after he had ordered me to attention, he hit me in the face with clenched fists as hard as he could. He knocked me down many times and I became very dazed. Whilst on the ground he kicked me in the stomach, on my back and shins. Every time I rose he tried to knock me down again. Finally, he ordered me back to camp and as I hobbled away with aching body and swollen face, he tripped me to the ground and gave me a few more kicks. I was boiling with rage, but knew that to defend myself might mean death. One of the things we had to learn was to take a bashing from these creatures and be absolutely passive, show no fear, try and remain on our feet, and hope that one day our turn would come.

Chapter 14

Trains and Pigs

"Time does his work honestly, and I don't mind him. But care and suffering are devils who tread down the brightest flowers and do more harm in a month than Time does in a year."
                                                                Charles Dickens

Before our arrival for "Yasumi" at Wun Lun there were only sixty men in the camp and they had been employed on rice carrying. Sacks of the stuff had to be humped from stores near the river to the railway line for despatch up country and after a few days we were given this job also. The sacks weighed about a hundred kilos and had to be carried about three hundred yards. It was strenuous work that brought home to us our emaciated condition for though we carried but few sacks a day, it completely exhausted us. The few peanuts we stole from a nearby field supplied a little much needed vitamin B but not enough to make any real difference.

We took tobacco leaves from the plantation and found a way in which we could cure them and so keep up our supply of smokes. There were kapok trees here too, unfortunately not enough for us to make use of their produce. We could certainly have done with some of it to at least make decent pillows, a little softer than one's army mess tin. All the same I was fascinated when these large pods burst and to see their contents drift to the ground like so much fine snow or confetti.

Soon after our arrival at Wun Lun the first steam train passed cautiously through the station, and so defeated the argument we had maintained, "They'll never be able to run real trains on this lousy railway." Daily parties of men fresh from Changi and other parts of Singapore passed through by train, actually being transported in trains gingerly running on the track we had built so far! They were going up to continue the railway further towards Burma, we were told. We were also made aware that after a short spell of "rest" we would be joining them.

Our numbers were swelled by another thousand men from Chungkai and our party started work on the line once more. A variation in our tasks this time. We had to lift parts of the rails by jacks and crowbars and bang ballast under the sleepers with a special type of pick. To hit the sleeper instead of the ballast brought the certainty of a bashing from a Nip. We were levelling, reinforcing and strengthening the line now that several heavy engines and trains had caused it to settle. We replaced rails, carrying them by the same method we had used building bridges, men either side holding poles passed under the rail, moving slowly, encouraged frequently by a bamboo across the back. Perhaps the work could be described as being very much the same as that which a British platelayer might do, but ours somewhat more crudely, and carrying with it the prospect of blows for every mistake made.

Wet or fine, the Nips kept us hard at it. If it poured with rain they had their oilskin clothes; while the sun blazed down they contrived to stand in the shade and shout their orders, the most common of which was "Speedo." We had nothing to wear but ragged shorts or loincloths.

These loincloths were called "Jap Happies" because the Nips wore them instead of underpants. Originally British wearers had been known as "Jap Happy", because they imitated the Nips. It was also a term of reproach signifying willingness to curry favour with our detestable captors. Our recognised clothing was now, however, a past luxury. "Jap Happies" were becoming the only clothing we possessed.

We made them from any odd piece of shirt or cloth. The material would be torn into a rectangular shape perhaps three feet long and six to eight inches wide. If one was lucky the cloth might be stitched with a hem, but more often than not left rough. Cord or tape was fastened to either side at one end and this taken round the waist and tied leaving the material hanging down the back. The Jap Happy would then be brought up through the legs and tucked through the tape or string tied on one's stomach; a very simple loin cloth affording some degree of modesty.

Our footwear by this time was almost non-existent, many chaps were walking about bare-footed, I hadn't quite reached this stage, my boots were almost completely worn out but I had been able to wire on the soles to make them last a little longer.

At first the food, by previous standards, was fairly good at Wun Lun, but with the arrival of the additional men, our rations became very small. We still had our jungle stew, mostly water with the odd trace of vegetable, but the quantity of rice was almost halved. Consequently it was with real eagerness that four of us answered "yes" to the Nip enquiry "Anybody know how to kill pigs?"

Well, Snub did. He was a butcher in civilian life and the other three of us could help. Our experience wouldn't amount to much but we could learn. Jack had been a bus driver after retiring from the boxing profession. "Samples," well, he was a bit of a mystery. We couldn't quite make out his former occupation. His only proved capacity was to tell the story of how he'd been out with a girl in Newcastle and left it too late to return to camp so asked her to sleep with him in a hotel. She agreed on condition he wore his long army pants as his legs were so rough! I was a postman, but there, you don't need a university education to tell you that if you kill pigs for the Nips, you can steal quite a lot of the animal to fill your hungry stomachs.

"Go on, have a bash Snub," we urged when he objected that it might be a Nip Tobang job (batman) up-country.

"Think of the steak and chops."

"Well, there'll be the guts," said Snub thoughtfully, "the Nips won't want them. Could we use them do you think?"

Could we? We'd show him. Down to the enclosure we went and dragged the poor pig to a hole in the ground which was to serve as the slaughterhouse.

"Blimey, look at its bloody rice belly," said "Samples". It was colossal and dragged on the ground. We thought of the fat we should get for frying.

We turned the wretched creature on its back, Jack and I sat on its belly while "Samples" stood by with a bucket to catch the blood. The pigs head was stretched back and its jaws held tightly together muffling the fearful squealing just a bit. Snub soon proved that his meek and mild behaviour and perpetual grin concealed his skill as a butcher. In went the knife piercing the vital artery and out spurted the blood. "Samples" caught most of this in his bucket, stirring it the whole time with his arm to prevent it congealing. That blood was going to the cookhouse to make us a black pudding.

"Never mind the humane killer you had in civvy street, Snub," we told him as he pumped the animal's foreleg to assist the flow of blood, "You're doing fine."

The unfortunate pig was now quite dead and we lifted the carcase onto a bamboo platform for Snub to scrape it using boiling water from the cookhouse. This done, we hung the carcase on a bamboo frame and Snub got busy cutting it up. Out came the guts, lights and chunks of fat into "Samples" waiting pail. Off we went to wash our booty in the river. This proved no easy job as the fish were most aggressive and tried to snatch it from us.

Later that day Jack and I made a fire at the end of our hut and boiled our ill gotten gains in an old four gallon tin that we normally used for washing purposes. Snub and Willie, meanwhile, were rendering down great lumps of fat from which we hoped to obtain sufficient oil to meet all our frying needs for the next few days.

Some time after, "Samples" wiped his mouth appreciatively on the back of his hand, "That won't stay inside us long enough to do any good," he remarked. "It will be a straight through job, Speedo Benjo!" He was right, the rich fat was too much for us and while we enjoyed the unaccustomed taste of meat, our bodies were not in a condition to assimilate nourishment. However, Snub must have made a good impression on our masters, he retained the dubious position of butcher until the remaining few animals were slaughtered, then we had to scheme up another means of supplementing our rations, we did, by boiling dhal beans pinched from the local Nip store.

It was becoming very difficult to get a haircut or shave, many men grew beards but we were fortunate to have in our party, Snowy, the Sergeant with very blond hair and prepared to have a go at anything. It was he who recovered all those buckets from the well at Ban Pong. Snowy still possessed a cut throat razor, not too sharp, but anyone prepared to risk his methods could have facial growth removed once a week. Snowy was no barber, he worked like the rest of us and unselfishly became "Snowy Todd" in his yasumi hours. He was always in a hurry. It was frightening to see him wielding his razor, almost everything came off, with each stroke; hairs, dirt and often the odd piece of skin.

My diarrhoea became quite out of control. Nothing seemed to make any difference so I ate everything that was going! I was rapidly getting thinner and weaker. Oh! the journeys from the hut to the latrines at night! The huts were becoming dilapidated, and tumbledown. The ground surface, uneven through constant use, was covered in filthy muck when wet. Inside the huts was almost as bad and even more hazardous at night. Bumping against every obstacle, falling over in the mud, stubbing a toe on a protruding root, and failing to reach the latrine in time. Hardly a night passed without my having to leave "Jap Happy" or shorts outside the hut ready to be washed in the morning.

To add to my misery small ulcers grew on my swollen ankles and legs. They were washed twice a day and painted with mercurochrome, but there were no bandages to cover them so the sores became swarming grounds for flies which pestered and bit continuously. Here, medical supplies were practically nil, but some of us similarly afflicted, found one way to get the sores cleaned. We would lie with our legs in the river and let the fish nibble off the scabs. Sores and scabs were their speciality. A few yards down stream the same cannibal fish became tasty food for the fishing Nips!

Towards the end of April instructions were received that another working party was required to go up country. Travel would be by train followed by a ten day march, but this time a number of sick men would be excused. It was the same old story, the Nips demanded that only the very sick remain. By this time I was down to about seven stone, having lost five and a half stone of my normal weight. I was getting so weak and thin that it was no surprise to me to find myself excluded from this working party. After the usual inspection, to weed out the sick, I was told that I would be going in the opposite direction, hopefully to receive some sort of treatment and rest. I didn't want to leave my pals in the Cambridgeshire Regiment, but accepted the good advice and in doing so probably saved my life. And so on the 5 May 1943, with a number of other sick men, I was put into a railway truck to start the short journey to Tamarkan.

"I built this bloody railway. Like hell I did. Look at the state of my legs!"

Chapter 15

Tamarkan

"It is not death, but dying, which is terrible."
Henry Fielding
1707–1754

The journey by train was uneventful, if one didn't count the sparks from the engine that fell among us in our open truck. The engines were fuelled by wood, perhaps not as effective as coal, but cheap and in plentiful supply beside the embankment. As we went down the line I was amazed to see that the jungle had reclaimed all the land we had cleared. Even the holes dug to obtain soil for the embankment had become filled, and the embankment itself green with vegetation. We passed through the now completed quarry at Chungkai, and were soon passing over a wide river on a wooden bridge about two hundred yards long. POW's were working erecting the steel bridge alongside it. Over the river and we were in Tamarkan station where we disembarked.

The term station may convey a false impression of what most of these places were like. This one consisted of a small atap building and siding, and was typical of what they were like at the time. Within a few minutes we were at the entrance to Tamarkan camp and found it sited some two hundred yards from the river and completely fenced in with bamboo. A Nip guardroom was at the entrance and from my immediate impression it appeared the cleanest POW camp I'd seen.

The Nips in charge of our sick party had the greatest difficulty in persuading their guards to admit us, but eventually we were taken in and paraded in front of the huts. We were counted innumerable times before the English officer, a Colonel Toosey, Commandant under the Nips, was allowed to address us. The Nips here were certainly very fussy and thorough.

DEE

Chungkai cutting, a section where the route of the railway had been cut through solid rock by 'slave' labour.

"This camp," the Colonel said, "is the cleanest in Thailand and I want you to keep it so. There has been very little illness here and only nine deaths in as many months. Now that it is to be a sick camp, keep it clean and disease will be kept under control. The Nips here are bastards. Discipline is very strict. Here are their orders and it will pay you to obey them:

> No smoking is allowed outside the huts.
> No sing-songs or lectures are permitted.
> All games are banned, also books.
> Nobody must go within two metres of the perimeter fence.
> All Nips must be saluted and you must stand when they enter the huts."

We learned the orders the hard way by seeing or taking the beatings that came from breaking them. The Colonel received many a clout himself from trying to save us from the savage punishment the Nips handed out daily. They were swine. They just had to hit somebody. I was put into a hut that had been selected to take ulcer cases. Very few of us at first but our numbers rapidly increased. I should think we were the first occupants of the hut for some time because it was alive with bugs. They had a wonderful time feeding on us for the first few nights until we got the better of them. As soon as we laid on the bamboo slats they started biting and continued all night, sleep was almost impossible, the number I squashed between my fingers during the first few hours ran well into double figures.

The food was not too bad at first, the usual rice and vegetable stew, but it got steadily worse as the camp's numbers were constantly growing and the rations always in arrears. In spite of this many of us began to improve as we received some sort of treatment each day, and a visit from the MO every third. Treatment amounted to nothing more than having the ulcers scraped out and cleaned twice a day, very painful. Sometimes with a bit of luck, we might get a clean dressing. At least we were able to rest and no doubt this contributed as much to our recovery as the scanty medication. We were constantly being inoculated for rat-plague, dysentery and cholera.

The last named terrified us all as we knew it had broken out up country. I heard that my unit had been badly hit, but the names and details at this time were unknown.

Of all the diseases we were likely to contract there is no doubt that cholera was the most feared. It was possible for a man to be reasonably fit in the morning, catch cholera, and be dead before the evening. Everyone became more fly conscious than usual. Killing them was top priority, should one land on one's food, the meal would not be eaten. We had always been careful about water, never drinking it without it first being boiled, now it was necessary to be extremely careful how one washed.

All victims dying from cholera had to be burned and the Nips kept well out of the way. The men carrying out the cremations had a grim and dangerous task, they were very prone to catch the disease themselves, in spite of being sprayed with dubious strength disinfectant.

More than one eye witness told how the occasional body would move and attain a sitting position, as the heat of the funeral pyre contracted the dead man's muscles. Sights that remain in one's memory for ever.

It was said that one of our chaps was nearly dead from the disease and that the Nips ordered him to be shot to prevent the disease from spreading. The guard detailed to do the job was so scared of catching the disease that his rifle shook in his hands, and it was obvious he would wound the patient any number of times before killing him. In the end a British officer took the rifle and despatched the sufferer. The Nips immediately arrested him for murder but we were told he was subsequently discharged.

All new admissions to Tamarkan were sprayed with disinfectant from head to foot before they were allowed to enter the camp. Eating utensils were dipped into boiling water before meals, disinfectant was at the end of every hut and we dipped our hands in it before entering. No man dared to put a cigarette to his lips if his fingers had touched the tip. Men were now coming down from the jungle in a continuous stream. Some died on the way, some at the very gates of the camp, and many of those who got in were like skeletons and died within a few days. Our numbers had now risen to nearly a thousand and were increasing all the time.

There were only fifty medical orderlies to attend this ever increasing number of sick men and several ex-patients who were on the mend, I among them, volunteered to act as orderlies.

For several years before the war I had been a member of St Johns Ambulance Brigade, and felt there might be some small contribution I could make. God knows there was a desperate need for anyone willing and able to have a go. Most of my ulcers had cleared quite quickly and the MO had found a cure for my diarrhoea – several spoonfuls of crushed charcoal taken with water each day. Not very pleasant, both the consuming and the end result causing a great deal of amusement to my fellow prisoners, but it did the trick.

POW's with the gruesome task of burning the bodies of their comrades, victims of one of the outbreaks of Cholera.

CHARLES THRALE

Chapter 16

Medical Orderly

"There is a remedy for all things but death, which will be sure to lay us flat some time or another."

Cervantes

I was put to work in the ulcer ward which now housed about two hundred men, mostly British and Australian. Very few Dutchmen seemed to get ulcers, but there were any number of them in the beri beri and dysentery wards, and it was there that most of the deaths occurred during the first few weeks.

The ulcers were mostly on ankles and legs and the ward stank of rotting flesh. Some were as big as three inches in diameter and as soon as the bandages were taken off flies swarmed all over them. We had to bathe the ulcers twice a day but had no new dressings to cover them, the old ones had to be scraped clean of green slimy puss, washed in a bucket and replaced. Our hands reeked so much that we dreaded meals until we got used to even that putrid stench. Neglect of dressing and cleaning the ulcers for one day meant the growth in size of at least half an inch. It was just as if something was eating the flesh away leaving green and black rotten tissue behind.

I was taken off my job as general ward orderly and given one man to look after. Looking nearly dead, he was filthy dirty, eyes staring from sockets almost hidden by protruding cheek-bones, he looked like a skeleton covered with scaly skin. He couldn't have weighed more than five stone but must have been at least six feet tall. He was a Dutchman and had just arrived with a party that day. He lay face downwards on a stretcher midst several days motions caused by his acute diarrhoea.

There were three large ulcers on his back, one between his shoulder blades over an inch deep. They were all full of big fat wriggling white maggots. I cleaned his ulcers, removing as many maggots as I could get hold of with a small pair of forceps, cleaned up his excreta and gave him a wash. From somewhere I scrounged a clean stretcher. Four days I looked after this Dutchman, continually cleaning him up. If I left him for just a few minutes he would call out for me. He died on the fourth night, poor devil.

With the death of this man I was given another job, this time to look after the three worst ulcer cases in the ward. The Medical Officer, an Australian named Major Moon, told me in confidence that he would have to amputate the legs in the next few days, but if I worked hard and followed his instructions there was just a chance of saving them. The first was a man from Suffolk "Tug Wilson", a member of the Royal Artillery. He had a very bad ulcer on the front of his leg ten inches long by four inches across, six inches of shin bone was exposed and the whole area a filthy black green colour. The next was a Dutchman with one almost the same size, but on the calf of his leg. It reached from the bend of his knee to his

An impression of the ulcer 'ward' at Tamarkan.

Charle's Thrale's impression of an operation in the jungle at one of the camps 'up country'.

ankle. The third, another Englishman, with a hideous looking ulcer eating away his instep, leaving bones exposed as they reached towards his toes, the next part of the unfortunate's foot waiting to be devoured by the detestable, greedy abomination.

I did work hard and continuously on these men until they began to dread my visits. By bathing them for twenty minute periods and removing dead flesh with scissors and forceps the ulcers became much cleaner. The Dutchman's leg and the Englishman's foot ulcers were held in check and in places showed signs of healing. The ulcer of the Suffolk man did not respond, in fact another developed on the back of his leg, and in no time had joined up with the one on the front. The rest of the leg became three times its normal size and the patient too weak to even sit up.

The MO decided to amputate, it was the leg or the man's life.

This was the first amputation to be performed in Tamarkan and the MO asked me if I would like to assist. The operation was carried out in an improvised theatre, nothing more than an area at the end of one of the bug ridden huts, a disgusting place at the best of times. Bamboo with an atap roof, half sides made of the same material. Mother nature's bare earth – a dusty floor. No gowned, capped and masked surgeons here, supported by an entourage of nurses and assistants. No spotlessly clean operating tables and powerful overhead lights. Just a couple of bamboo slatted tables, several buckets, improvised instruments and two very dedicated, conscientious but overworked medical officers, and a couple of us orderlies barefooted and clad in our loin cloths. The unfortunate patient on the table, hopefully sufficiently drugged to withstand the trauma of having his leg sawn off, a tourniquet in position on his thigh and the medical officer speedily got down to the serious business in hand.

A swift half moon action with his scalpel and he deftly laid back the outer skin as one would peel an orange. This would become a flap to bring down and stitch over an inevitable mass of raw flesh.

The scalpel then cut deeper into the leg and as the incision was made, locking forceps clipped on to the ends of the main arteries and veins. When the bone was reached it became my job to steady the leg whilst another pair of hands, smothered in blood, encompassed the lower part of the wound in an endeavour to pull back the flesh, along the bone, sufficiently far for the Major to get to work with his hacksaw blade and hew through the femur. It didn't take long, thank God, before the leg was off and the remaining stump left slightly elevated several inches from the bench, one mass of bloody flesh, several pairs of forceps dangling from the severed veins and arteries. The ends of these blood vessels were swiftly tied, checks made to ensure that excess bleeding had ceased and the forceps removed.

The area was swabbed, cleaned and in a very short time the spare outside skin brought down and stitched leaving a tidy looking stump ready for bandaging.

I was impressed!

It fell to my lot to take away the unwanted limb for disposal. My, how heavy it seemed. I hoped that its removal would lead to a speedy recovery of the amputee. It did! The patient recovered quickly once the leg was off, soon put on weight and began hobbling about on a pair of crutches made from bamboo. The other Englishman recovered slowly and did not lose his leg, but the Dutchman wasn't so lucky. After making what looked like great progress over a five week period, his ulcer became rapidly worse and nothing but amputation of the leg could save him. The operation took place and seven days later he too was stomping about the camp on his bamboo crutches.

After these amputations many more followed, some men recovered but unfortunately many died too. It seemed impossible to check the ulcers, they grew at a tremendous rate, completely out of control.

In many cases gangrene set in and hardly a day passed without a death in the ulcer ward. It became known as the "Slaughter house" because of the cries of pain from the patients as their ulcers were being cleaned and dressed. It was often said, throughout the camp, that anyone getting into the ulcer ward never came out alive. Unfortunately men with large ulcers were naturally very weak, and prone to catch any of the many other diseases that were rampant all the time.

In the other wards the death rate was also high, malnutrition and beri beri claimed their victims, some swollen like balloons by fluid caused by wet beri beri, and others shrivelled into warped skeletons from the other extreme. Dysentery and cerebral malaria were the causes of many deaths. It was nothing unusual to hear men moaning and delirious from cerebral malaria, then to become quiet, and within an hour or so be carried out dead. Sheer exhaustion, starvation and despair accounted for many lives.

In fact death became such an everyday occurrence that men took little or no notice when the man laying beside him died.

Many of my friends were returning from work on the railway in the most pitiful condition. They brought news of many lads who had died and been buried or burnt near the line. One Cambridgeshire came to help me in the ulcer ward and had the misfortune to have a scratch on his hand in which ulcerous matter settled, a terrific ulcer developed and after a most painful time the hand healed, only to be useless and crippled for life. It was typical of these ulcers. They were horrible evil things. A little prick from a sharp piece of bamboo, followed by a slight irritation, without thinking a scratch from a dirty finger nail and that was it. Next day a sore the size of a shirt button and within a week an ulcer three inches across and half an inch deep.

After a time rations improved and a "special" diet was arranged for the very sick men. Several men risked their lives in night expeditions to break out of camp and meet Thais, returning with medical supplies and equipment. As if by magic, men began to recover from various complaints and wasted skeleton like bodies began to fill out. And there was also a small drop in the death rate too. In order to obtain supplies from the natives, men had robbed a Nip store and were taking the tools out to sell. There is no doubt that not all their transactions were to benefit the camp, they were also looking after themselves.

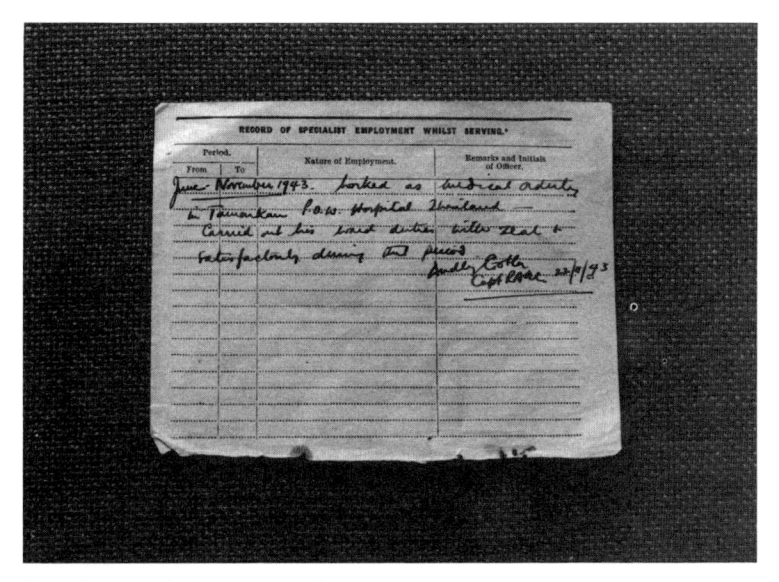

Page from pay book. Entry made in my new army pay book when it was issued upon my release. Captain Gotla thought that my assistance in the 'ulcer ward' was worthy of a mention.

Unfortunately, several of them were caught by the Nips who sent for the Kempies, the notorious military police. They beat and tortured these men for nearly a fortnight, stripping them naked and beating them on all parts of the body with bamboo, forcing them to drink water until blown up like balloons and jumping on them until the water ran out. Cries of agony rang in our ears day after day until, eventually, the victims were taken off to Singapore Military Prison.

While in Tamarkan we were allowed to send another card home, but better still received our first mail, not everyone was lucky, this was October 1943 and I had two short letters written in June the previous year.

Tamarkan was changing from being the place of complete restriction and harsh discipline and becoming quite a decent camp, if compared with what we had found on arrival. Football was being played some evenings and various other sporting activities allowed. Under Nip escort bathing was allowed in the river. Concerts took place once a week and during the entertainment, we were allowed the privilege of smoking outside the huts. After the hopeless, dispiriting experience of disease and death, the comparative cheerfulness was a great tonic to us.

Chief among our entertainers was Bobbie, a private in the Royal Army Ordnance Corps. I had first seen him playing the part of a female impersonator at Changi. It was he who played the part of the "Jungle Princess" in the entertainment at our first Christmas as prisoners. Little did I think then that he and I would be orderlies together in an ulcer ward, or that we would be roughing it side by side in the same bug ridden hut.

He was an extraordinary fellow and so completely feminine in his habits that I often found him most embarrassing. He carried a full set of ladies attire with him and for his stage appearances would wear a complete women's rig-out, roll on corsets and all. It amazed me how he had managed to keep it all and carry it about with him, because apart from his entertainment appearances he was like the rest of us, "Jap Happy" or tattered shorts and precious little else.

The Nips would come round to see his dresses. I think more than one fancied him in his female attire. He would spend a great deal of time over his teeth and hair, talked like a girl – "Oh dear, mother's tired," being his favourite phrase – and was a dab hand at mending clothes. He kept a folder of "cuttings" which told of his appearances on stage and for every show made out a programme with his own name on top of the bill.

He would do individual turns in the wards. "I'm an old Norman Castle with a ruined tudor wing," is one that sticks in my mind. When he shaved his hairy chest and legs, and dressed as a woman it was difficult to believe he wasn't the genuine article. I've known him sit on patients' beds looking so much like a woman, that they would blush and attempt to cover their nakedness. I could understand their feelings for I myself, who knew him so well, often felt most awkward in his company. He starred in a number of shows in several of the larger camps. They were always enthusiastically received by prisoners, usually being brilliantly produced by Leo Britt, a Corporal in the RASC, who had been a professional actor in civilian life. Poor Bobbie, he later died at sea on a ship bound for Japan. I have often felt since, that had he not been so embarrassingly feminine, we would have shown much more gratitude for his attempt to cheer a most dismal stretch of our time as prisoners.

It was now several months since I had arrived at Tarmarkan a very sick man. As a result of being made a hospital camp, Tamarkan had become home to men from many different camps and Regiments. We were a mixed bunch. Since my recovery to somewhat normal prison camp health, I had been sharing sleeping quarters with men from several different regiments, including ROAC and Royal signals, but no Cambridgeshires. Someone decided, I suppose it must have been the Nips, that we should be re-grouped into our original working battalions. Chungkai was destined to become the camp for Number Two Group, and as I belonged to that formation I knew it was only a matter of time before I was sent to Chungkai again.

I didn't look forward to it. In spite of being separated from many of my colleagues, I had been reasonably happy here. The ulcer ward with its stench, cries of agony and deaths was bad enough, but I felt I had been making some contribution towards easing the suffering of at least a few fellow prisoners.

Chapter 17

Back to Chungkai

"If people are fit to live, let them live under decent human conditions. If they are not fit to live, kill them in a decent way."
George Bernard Shaw
1856–1950

The sick men were taken first by transport, and the end of October found me once more, marching along the railway track bound for Chungkai. Arrived there, I found the place grown out of all recognition. Many more huts had been built and the hospital area alone was bigger than the camp I had left the year before. Jungle had been cleared right back and the cemetery, which had been some distance away, was now within the camp perimeter. On arriving we were counted, re-counted and eventually allocated huts and places to sleep. There may have been more huts, but there were many more men also, and the numbers were increasing daily.

In the hut to which I was sent we were shoulder to shoulder, a space about eighteen inches wide per man. The hospital was so appalling that it made Tamarkan seem like heaven. Huts were falling down, dark and filthy dirty. In one hut alone I counted forty men with only forty legs between them. All having lost limbs, they looked thin, haggard and many had lost the will to live. Here and there a poor wretch gasped his last breath, while others with terrific ulcers were awaiting amputation.

The Beri Beri wards were full of hideous living skeletons, thin wasted bodies, match-stick limbs and eyes staring from sunken sockets. It was hard to imagine that fit troops, mostly men in their early twenties, could through slavery, bad food and disease, become such wrecks in just over a year. The death rate had been as high as twenty a day and on our arrival there were at least six burials daily.

An impression of one of the larger camps. Those 'down country' or base camps might hold up to 2,000 men. They were always of the same construction, bamboo and atap. In some of the smaller 'up country' camps, where the numbers involved could be anything between 50 and 200 men, the accommodation provided might amount to nothing or perhaps a few tents.

Two good friends from my home town were amongst the casualties. One was fellow occupant of the "Imperial Palace" down at River Valley, Singapore and the other, the officer who had asked me in the Regimental Aid Post, at the time of the fighting, "How about Royston now?" He was a good chap. It seemed ages ago since we were small boys together and I was the only one allowed to ride his little tricycle. When he was commissioned an estrangement set in – neither his fault nor mine. We were both stupidly aware of the difference in rank, and afraid to approach each other on the matter. However, all that broke down after we had seen action together and it was Ken and Jack as it used to be. Several times he slipped me a few dollars out of his officer's allowance, and did his utmost to make life more bearable for us other ranks.

Nearly every man in Chungkai was ill. Shadows of men walked about barefooted with a "Jap Happy" as the only item of clothing. They were covered in sores and had scaly powdery skin, just as though every spot of moisture had been drained from it. It was easy to pick out men arriving from Tamarkan, reduced to the same conditions regarding clothing and footwear, but skins were clearer and men looked fitter. That's as far as it went.

Very little work was being done, in fact there were very few fit men to do it. I joined a working party and the jobs we did were mainly hut building and gardening.

Some of the sick men, not confined to their beds were running small businesses, or rackets, from goods they had secured by breaking out of camp at night and bargaining in the nearby kampongs. They brought back mainly tobacco and sacci, a native brewed whisky, selling at profit to those willing and able to buy. Cigarette "factories" were run by groups of six or eight men and their products hawked round the camp at five cents a bundle, each bearing their own trade names, "Nobbies," "Plus Twos," "Harvest Gold," and "Drum Major".

Nip restrictions were less severe than those we had found on arrival at Tamarkan. Nightly, lectures were given in the huts on subjects ranging from "Christian Science" by the Padre to "Experiences of the Criminal" by men who had done time before war service and becoming our fellow prisoners. All manner of men were encouraged to take part, it was one way of relieving the boredom and men discovered talents they never thought they possessed.

Lectures were liable to be interrupted by a Nip guard nicknamed "Ash Tray Charlie" who would beat up any man smoking without a tin lid of water beside him as an ashtray. Word would soon be passed round that he was on the prowl, and it was seldom that he was able to catch anybody offending his own regulation.

Concerts were held nearly every week, I saw several good shows, most of the cast being made up of officers, many playing female parts and making a good job of it too. Costumes were made from old rags and strips of useless mosquito nets, dyed by various ingenious methods and looking very effective from short distances.

It should be pointed out that I saw no ordinary prisoner in possession of a mosquito net during the whole time I was prisoner, perhaps officers had them, I don't know. In one or two of the bigger camps the Nips issued large green ones which would provide limited protection for seven or eight men, even then, ninety per cent of the camp were without. It was these large nets which eventually became props for the stage shows.

Bedding was almost non-existent. A rice sack made a good blanket if one could be scrounged. Many men were without this form of luxury. We would lay at night waving off mosquitoes and killing the occasional lice or bug, until exhausted we would lapse into sleep and allow all three categories of blood suckers to eat their fill.

Food was in short supply and very poor. Breakfast was now "pap", rice that had been boiled until it became like porridge and was almost inedible, even with the spoonful of sugar we sometimes had. I loathed the stuff. The midday meal was still jungle stew which was repeated in the evening, but with the addition of a "dufor". Nobody seemed to know how this name originated but it stayed as long as we were prisoners. One version was that the cook once said "that will do for them!" and the term was adopted. It was rice baked or fried in the shape of a cup with a sweet or savoury filling – it was always hard to tell which.

I was hungry all the time and nearly every night would dream of being at home enjoying a really good meal, only to awake in the morning as hungry as ever, and finding the same sloppy pap for breakfast. I suppose I might have dreamt of the fair sex had I the strength, it was a couple of years since we had seen one. My only eating utensil, a spoon, had broken in half and it now had a bamboo handle. Drink on rare occasions was very weak tea minus sugar and milk, sometimes a coffee made from burnt rice but most times just plain hot water. Hot because it was always boiled before drinking, coming from the river it had to be.

The shortage of food led to "Leggi" queues and Leggi, as we

understood it, was the Malay word for "more". Something that was introduced by the Dutchman. After drawing their food some men would immediately form another queue waiting to get any rice that was left over after everybody had been served. If there were sick men in your hut you were lucky in leggi queues. Sick men rarely drew their full share of rice. It was common to see some men going to other unit feeding points and scraping out the rice containers after the men at that point had finished their meal.

Bamboo carrying was a racket that interested some. The possession of a Nip tally allowed men out of the camp to collect bamboo from the jungle for the cookhouse fires, and five cents a load was the reward, with leggis. The money and food wasn't easily earned, we had to tramp three or four kilometres in bare feet through thorny jungle but it did provide the opportunity to make contacts outside, and perhaps get the odd snippet of news.

My second Christmas as a prisoner, like the first, was spent in Chungkai but this time without the dysentery. In fact I was feeling fairly fit and thus able to enjoy the little extra that our messing money had been able to procure for the "Festivities". A considerable part of our paltry earnings were taken each week to help supplement the Nip ration issue, I never knew how much or if we had full benefit from it, God knows the food was bad enough, but we did have a special effort made that Christmas Day.

Breakfast was a fried egg, the first I'd had in over a year, plain rice and sweet tea. Midday, rice and a little fried veg plus a second course of sweetened rice. In the evening, rice, fried pumpkin slice, a small piece of meat, sweet potato and green vegetable cooked separately, followed by a baked rice, "Christmas Cake" Dufor. There was even coffee and a baked rice short bread later in the evening!

I attended the church service which was held in the cemetery, where nearly two thousand of our men had been buried. In the evening there was a concert, entertainment from the Chungkai stars.

The Nips used to hold a complete check roll call about every ten days or so, and relied on the units to hold their own night and morning parade, the resultant figures being handed in daily to the Nip office. They did however spring additional unannounced searches and roll calls at frequent intervals, the searches were more thorough. We would all be turned out while they checked all the hut and kits, they took away such things as pencils, knives and any paper resembling a diary or map. They never did find everything,

Back to Chungkai

quite often items were buried or hidden in various parts of the camp away from the huts.

New Years Day arrived. Although sports were organised there were very few men anywhere fit enough to take part. The most successful feature was the race meeting with Tote and bookmakers complete. The larger men were the horses and the smaller, jockeys. Every horse was named and considerable excitement generated. I was feeling much fitter and allowed myself to be entered as a horse with another Cambridgeshire to be my jockey. We were fancied and heavily backed by our pals. They lost their money however, as I tripped and fell ten yards from the start. Actually I was far from fit, and a small ulcer on my leg developed into something else and a fortnight later found me in hospital with a leg swollen to twice its normal size. The pain was excruciating and walking impossible.

I entered the surgical ward and found that many of my fellow patients were those I had been attending at Tamarkan. The MO in charge had been there too. In a fortnights stay I got used to the sights and smells around me and could marvel at the improvised bed pans, bottles, leg-rests and crutches all made out of bamboo. Many legs had been amputated but a number of ulcers had been cut completely out, and by this method some very large ones were being healed. They were even having limited success with skin grafts, taking little snippets off backsides and transferring them to healing areas on legs. A team of masseurs were doing wonders with deformed limbs but scarcely a day passed without a death.

The hospital had a separate cookhouse and the food much better than that in the lines, every effort was being made by the British Administration to give priority to the sick, improve their health and cut down the number of deaths.

When I was discharged from Hospital I expected to be fit for work, or at least return to work in a few days, but it was not so. Instead I joined the already large number of those "sick in lines". In a few days beri beri set in. It started with aching limbs and loss of appetite and I was soon hobbling about like a wasted old man. No matter what position I tried to rest in, the same aching continued day and night. The MO ordered me to eat as much rice polishings as possible.

I took six tablespoons of the unpleasant stuff everyday, but was not to see any change in my condition for several weeks. I dreaded the nights knowing that I would be unable to sleep, the day light hours were almost as bad, my hands trembled and I reached the stage when I thought I was losing my sanity. It was over three months before there was any noticeable improvement, when sure enough I realised I was on the way to recovery. My appetite improved, I was managing to sleep more, walk better and my hands ceased to tremble.

How much luckier I was than some of the chaps. I thought this one day when I was forcing the rice polishings down my throat.

"Your pal Bill Evans has just died."

So he'd gone at last. He had been dying for a long time, I knew that and I'm sure he did too. I had met Bill again, in hospital, a couple of months before, after not seeing him for over a year. When I left Changi for Thailand, he had remained behind, coming up later and being sent to a different section of the railway. I visited the hospital huts when I returned to Chungkai looking for anyone I might know, and had passed by Bill, until he called out, "Don't you remember an old pal, Jack?" Frankly I didn't recognise him and would have seen him as just another dying man, had he not spoken.

I had only looked in on him this morning and seen him lying on his bamboo platform, a sack to lie on and a patched blanket for cover, asleep with his eyes wide open. What a contrast he was to the spruce, fair haired young man that the girls would fall for at the dances we attended in England. My age, twenty three years old, he looked like an old man of eighty. His blond hair was matted and lifeless, the skull-like face covered with stubble, the head looked grotesque on that wasted frame, just a skeleton covered with skin, if one could call it skin, all covered with sores and scales that powdered on the slightest touch. His knee joints were set at absurd angles, and he only had little use in one hand, the other was shrivelled and useless, the result of continuous sores.

He was typical of many prisoners at that time, doomed to die but determined not to give up. I'd go to re-read his letters for him but he would fall asleep before I finished, and I learned afterwards that the "dufors" I took he gave away after I left. Poor Bill. He had a widowed mother, his father had been killed in the first world war. Now she had lost her only son, what a shocking waste it all was, and in what terrible circumstances to die.

Of course, I'd go to the funeral. I broke out of camp to get a little greenery from the jungle for a make shift wreath.

Later that day I paraded with a dozen or so men from various units and waited for bearers to bring along the corpses. Four men were being buried on this occasion. We followed them the short distance to the cemetery, fellow prisoners stopped and stood to attention as our pathetic little party passed. Not so the Nip guards. Changing at the time, they took not the slightest notice, chattering to each other as they straggled along. After all there was nothing unusual in a POW burial party.

After the short service and Last Post I saluted the grave. There lay Bill's shrivelled and twisted body in a rice sack – my poor wreath was in keeping with the rest of the funeral furnishings! I couldn't help wondering if I should finish in the same way. Would my friends be saying, "Poor old Cossy, he wasn't a bad chap." "Wonder if he had a wife and kids?" I speculated if it was true that the army made a charge for a burial blanket, surely they wouldn't charge for a lousy rice sack?

"Hell, I expect its jungle stew for tiffin! . . ."

The railway line was now completed and most POW's began returning to their base camps. Only a few men were being left at camps along the line for general maintenance, cutting fuel for engines and similar sort of work. The Nips informed us that men were being sent to Japan and asked for volunteers. Only fit men would be taken. Having experienced death and disease for well over a year in Thailand some did volunteer hoping for something better, and, thinking that there was a faint chance of being picked up at sea by the Allies. Nonsensical medical inspections were held and several parties of one hundred, so called, fit men were formed. I didn't get as far as the inspection!

Before the parties left for Chungkai they were fitted out with clothing from various sources by the Nips. The variety of kit almost passed belief. There were native straw hats, all the same size, "Bangkok bowlers" we called them, shorts, slacks, tartan trousers and long white pants in lieu of trousers. Most received a pair of Nip rubber boots. Some had tunics, others army vests, whatever the garment, it was seldom the right size. These men would be seen, in places, by the civilian population and the Nips wanted to let the world see that they clothed their prisoners. But what clothing. The whole exercise had every hall mark of a large comic opera, and it certainly had the same effect on us. However, in spite of all the amusement caused, these fantastic garments were better than going about naked as those of us did who were left behind in Thailand.

A number of my friends were on these parties and life became even more miserable after their departure. Conditions on the ships were appalling, over crowded, men hoarded in holds like cattle, sick and so called fit men alike. The stench must have been disgusting, dysentery cases finding it impossible to visit a latrine. Men becoming dehydrated through lack of water. Added to these intolerable conditions, was the added danger of the ships being sunk by allied submarines. Some of us had discussed trying to get on one of these parties for that very reason, naturally not wanting to be sunk, but the optimistic thought of ships being intercepted and the prospect of gaining earlier freedom. Hundreds of men never reached Japan, they were lost at sea, my pal "Snub" the butcher among them.

Chapter 18

A Policeman in Chungkai

"A policeman's lot is not a happy one"

W S Gilbert

All the time I was regaining health and benefitting from a course of remedial PT, and to feel fit was nearly everything. No more was I forced to sit up at night hugging my aching limbs, and longing to mingle my snores with those around me, even glad of the slight relief to my loneliness afforded by Bill Hines's regular dash to the latrines. My appetite had returned and I was no longer giving away three parts of my rice to the fitter men, who hungrily waited to see if I would leave any.

But despite my renewed health, I was not prepared for the shock the Sergeant gave me.

"Jack, you're looking much better. What about joining the police?"

"All coppers are bastards," I replied, chanting the soldier's creed. I'd heard tales of MP's who were Jap Happy and never tired of getting their own men into trouble. I told the Sergeant this, and more.

"Blimey, you don't think I'm that sort of swine, do you?" he asked. "Think it over. No work for the Nips, walk about and get plenty to eat, just the job to help you get fit again."

I was not persuaded, told Robbo I wanted nothing to do with the idea and dismissed it from my mind.

A fortnight later when told to report to the RSM at the police hut, as quickly as possible, I wondered what on earth I had done wrong. Perhaps that cattie of wog weed I'd been given the other day was stolen property. The RSM said nothing when I arrived except "Shun. Right turn. Quick march. Left wheel. Halt. Right turn." And when I had recovered from this almost forgotten routine I found myself standing in front of a table, on the other side of which sat a bald headed man in shorts. The next few minutes were vague. He talked, I listened, and before I knew what it was all about I was outside. I had joined the Police! The following day I reported to the RSM to be made more respectable in appearance to conform with my dignity as an MP and received a pair of patched shorts, a patched shirt and a strip of red cloth with "MP" on it in white letters.

The boots I received had seen better days, nearly worn out and the soles wired on in several places. But real black leather! Probably belonged to some poor devil who had died. This was a great improvement, totally different to walking about barefooted. I polished the boots with a mixture of dirt and black soot scraped off the top of an old oil lamp. I cleaned a borrowed regimental cap badge with dust from the floor of the hut. No socks, but an old pair of putties to wear round my ankles. (Strips cut from these later proved to be a very effective method of patching my hat.) I began to feel like a soldier again.

The Nips paid policemen, worker's rates, so I was much better off. Several other men started with me. We received instructions and these general rules of conduct were impressed upon us:

1 Walk smartly, set an example to fellow POW's and help them remember there is such a person as the British Soldier.
2 Keep petty thieving from colleagues and similar offences under control.
3 Prevent men from getting into trouble with the Nips.

I must admit there was much to be said in support of all three of these objectives. The period of captivity over two years now, was taking its toll. Some men who used to be smart, taking pride in their personal appearance had become shadows of their former selves. They didn't bother to wash, looked dejected, hopeless, and in many cases had given up the will to live. The term used to describe a character adopting this attitude was "letting himself go." I overheard this said about me on one occasion, I don't think it was justified but it certainly made me determined to prove them wrong.

I discovered that the policemen were not so bad. They ignored minor offences, overlooked infringement of Nip rules as far as they could, and came down heavily on the men who stole kit and dying men's blankets. There were exceptions of course. To the odd one, MP meant "massive power," and he used it whenever he could.

Our number varied between twenty and thirty and one of the best of our party was George Slade. George was a regular Sergeant from the Gordon Highlanders, he had a sleek black moustache and a very sharp tongue. He was known as the "Count of Chungkai" by the reason of the possessive air he had when he swaggered around the camp. Off duty he would flick the ash from his cigarette with a delicate flourish of the forefinger, one could almost imagine a solid gold ashtray in place of the rusty old tin lid. Many men in camp disliked him, perhaps they were unable to stand his verbal attack. If he caught an offender doing wrong he would reward him with a lashing from his tongue on the spot. He considered a good talking to from him did more good than an extra week's fatigues. I believe it did!

Crawford was the very opposite. He would put men on charge at every opportunity, even to the extent of "pulling" a man who had saved his life when he had malaria up country. True the offender had been caught smuggling eggs and tobacco into camp to sell at a profit, but he had risked his neck to visit the nearby Kampong and deserved some consideration.

One of my first jobs, with several other men was to mingle with the washing party at the river, and prevent kit being stolen while men were in the water. It was a hopeless game as there were about a thousand at a time on the banks and in the water. I would strip and swim with the others, hoping that my own stuff would not be pinched and reduce me to the indignity of returning stark naked to the police hut.

Camp patrol was a pleasant duty, involving little more than looking as smart as possible and strolling where we wished round the camp. We used to visit any pals in hospital, always being careful to position ourselves in the right spot whenever a train went past, so that we could report the nature of its load to the RSM. The RSM was a good fellow despite his formidable appearance, six feet four inches in his socks and a moustache that matched his rank. He was a terror to wrong doers but it was generally admitted that his bark was worse than his bite. When he turned up in the morning with curt orders to the police to stand at various points, we knew without being told that a news bulletin was in course of preparation and we must warn of any approaching Nip.

There was a "canary" (radio receiving set) in Chungkai, but very few knew where it was hidden or from where it operated. I had a good idea of where it was, but like the others, had no intention of endangering the lives of the operators by being inquisitive. Severe penalties threatened anybody receiving or disseminating news so we waited for Captain Holder to come round the huts and tell us the latest. He was an ordinary looking bloke with spectacles, when walking round in his Jap Happy he looked no different than the rest of us. I understood that he had been a broadcaster on Shanghai radio. He would calmly stroll into a hut, a book under his arm and say, "Get the look-outs posted, and if any nosey little bugger comes along, I am lecturing you on the Fly Menace." There would be no rush or panic, men would quietly move nearer and listen intensely as he passed on the news, perhaps a couple of weeks old, but it would be genuine news so who cared. Our gratitude to this officer was equal to our admiration for him.

Six of us did night duty, working in pairs. Four slept while two did duty. One stayed at the police hut in case of trouble in the camp, and the other did a spell at the "no good house". This was composed of five cells, three feet six inches wide, six feet long and perhaps six feet high, and was made of tightly woven bamboo. While in these cells, for periods ranging from three to twenty eight days, the prisoners had no water for washing, no bedding, and no time out at all. A hole was scraped in the corner and this served as a latrine.

If a Nip soldier served a spell, as they sometimes did, a Nip sentry stood guard as well, otherwise they only made an inspection each hour to make sure that the POW was not being favoured by his own men. The food whilst in here was usually plain rice; salt and water, sometimes only one meal a day. As the food came from a POW cookhouse there would often be a little stew or fish hidden under the rice, but if a Nip happened to occupy the next cell, for perhaps getting drunk, the POW could be in luck. The Nip guards would invariably smuggle them food and cigarettes, the POW would get half the spoils to keep his mouth shut. The policeman outside found two hours of this disgusting and horrible so what on earth must it be like inside?

I was to live long enough to find out!

Incarceration in these cells was a Nip punishment in most cases, and whenever possible we smuggled blankets into the prison, but the British and Dutch Authorities did sentence some of their own men for various offences, such as selling quinine or drugs to the Thais. This certainly merited the no good house, as quinine was very scarce and the lack of it caused many deaths. One POW got twenty-one days in the cells for stealing the only microscope in the camp and taking it out to sell in a nearby Kampong. This was a despicable act and he was lucky to get away so lightly. That microscope was the only means we had of detecting malaria. Eventually it was recovered at great risk by MP's and others who broke camp at night to comb the neighbouring Kampongs.

When discharged from the no good house the worst offenders were detained in what we called the PDB or Preventative Detention Barracks. They had a comparatively easy time, becoming members of ordinary working parties, but at the end of the day being detained under the supervision of the police. One I remember was a Dutch Eurasion named Hokenstein, an inveterate thief, and according to the story, two murders to his name. One was supposed to have been a native over-friendly with his wife, and the other a rival taxi driver who was under-cutting his trade. His fellow countrymen warned us that he would stick a knife in our backs, given half a chance, but he always seemed too much of a coward to attempt violence.

In addition to having a Police Force, Chungkai was rapidly becoming a self-contained unit of POW's, like a small town or village. Many tools had been improvised and work shops set up in various locations. Empty containers provided work for tin smiths who used their skills making baking tins, cooking utensils and drinking mugs. An open air barbers shop in the centre of the camp provided haircuts and shaves at five cents a time if you were lucky. It was a delightful setting, in the shade of gigantic tamarind trees. All very professional, there was a row of several chairs within a small bamboo railed area. There were even lather boys and a cashier to take the money. "Mr Maxfactor" ran the salon and important customers were favoured with his personal attention. The whole thing was quite a racket. Other ranks waited in long queues to have their heads nearly torn off, whilst Officers, Senior NCO's and favoured customers, with perhaps more cash, received preferential treatment. A far cry from the efforts of Snowy and his terrible fast shaves, carried out after a hard days work on the line.

A carpenters shop made crosses for the cemetery and aids for use in the hospital. The camp centre also boasted the PRI, a canteen where small cooked dishes were bought by those having cash.

"Sambal" made and introduced by the Dutchmen was a very popular dish at five cents a time, it was very hot, consisting mainly of chillies.

Food had improved or perhaps it was our cooks becoming more efficient, they ground rice into flour and were now baking something that bore a resemblance to bread. We called it bread, and this, with a little thin watery jam, became our regular breakfast in Chungkai. A number of Red Cross parcels arrived from America, there was supposed to be an issue of one per man, but by the time they reached us it became one between six. Too many Nips had access to them on the way.

I smoked my first "Lucky Strike" since the voyage on the West Point and heard a new tune as well. In the general Red Cross issue for the camp were a couple of "gramophones" and a number of records, most of them very old tunes except for one. It seemed hard to realise that it was more than two years since we had heard a new tune, this one I'll never forget. It wasn't much, but it was new! "I've got spurs that jingle, jangle, jingle, as I ride merrily along!" It soon became a popular tune in the camp, but the words were changed to suit the occasion.

Hardly a day passed without the appearance of an allied plane. It was always too high to recognise any markings but used to hover around long enough to take stock of all it surveyed. We called it "Charlie" and looked forward to his visits. No Nip planes ever appeared to intercept or chase him away. Nightly visits from allied planes became quite common, they usually passed overhead as though following the course of the river. Sometimes we would hear the sound of bombing or guns. One night a raid produced much closer explosions and the following day we heard that another camp, Non Pladuk, had been bombed and there were British and Dutch casualties. The camp was sited near a large railway siding containing petrol, and ammunition stores, probably there in the hope that they wouldn't be bombed because of the proximity of POW's. Some planes dropped leaflets and although most of them were printed in Thai or Burmese, the odd one did have the comforting forecast "Hold tight! We're coming!" in English.

The Nips ordered that trenches be dug round the huts, and shelters dug for their use. Surely the tide was beginning to turn in our favour? A Nip MO started making a nuisance of himself, he was supposed to be a Doctor, but if he had any knowledge of medicine, it was never apparent to us. We knew him as "Nobby" the horse doctor. He issued orders that each working battalion was to be allowed a certain number of sick, irrespective of the state they were in. "Nobby's" categories were to be, "men in hospital', men "bed down in lines", half day workers, full day light workers and the rest heavy workers capable of anything available. Our MO's had an unenviable job, men who were completely unfit for any type of work were made to do some sort of task. MO's refusing to co-operate received beatings on the orders of Nobby. Parties were still returning from up country in shocking states, others were required to go. If enough couldn't be found, Nobby would inspect himself, he usually got them from somewhere.

The Police hut was near the Quarter Master's sleeping quarters and we were aroused one night by the sound of loud voices which were easily recognised as belonging to the QM, another English Officer, and a particularly objectionable Nip called Omitz. We had first come across this nasty piece of work at Wun Lun. He held some similar rank of Nip QM in those days, he was a pale, seedy looking individual and it was easy to believe the rumour that he hadn't long to live and was making the most of his remaining time by pitching into us. There were many of us to testify to the weight of blows dealt by this "dying" man's bamboo. But the amazing thing was the change that had come over Omitz. No longer an invalid, and no longer aggressive! He must have seen the light!

It was difficult to hear what Omitz said but the voice of Major Craig, the QM, was unmistakeable.

"I'm sorry for you little yellow bastards," he bawled. It was obvious that Sacci, the native whisky had been circulating freely.

"Why do our men whistle and grin? Why don't they wrap up and die? I'll tell you. It's because they know who's going to win this bloody war and it's not you, or Tojo." In a minute the QM took up the tale again with the question "Do you know Moonface?" Omitz evidently didn't know him by that name and there followed a grunting and screeching which was an excellent impersonation of a hated camp guard. Omitz understood. "Well there are seven thousand men in this camp ready to fight for the pleasure of slitting his throat."

This shook Omitz who could be heard asking, in his fairly good English, whether that would be his fate too.

"You might get away with it," came the reassuring reply, "But if anybody wants to ring your bloody neck I shan't stop 'em. And now you can . . . . off, I want to sleep."

But it wasn't always a case of listening and doing nothing. On one occasion, just after mid-night, the most blood curdling screams were heard coming from the direction of the camp latrines.

"Come on," said Bill, the other MP on duty with me, "somebody has gone mad, and is shoving his victim down the bore hole." "Blimey, what a death! Sweet vi – o – lets!" As we neared the latrines, figures could be seen struggling. We rushed to separate them. I grabbed one, and then realised who he was – Kokuba, the Nip commandant and two of his sentries! Now, what would happen! Lt Kokuba was in one of his drunken bouts, and less disposed than ever to overlook my mistake. He was furious at being interrupted in his favourite occupation of beating an underling, and bellowed for an explanation.

"Kempie," I blurted.

"Kempie, Canaro, Buggero, dammy, dammy," he raved, grabbing a torch from the sentry and scanning us closely in its light.

"Kempitana, dammy, dammy, buggero, Kempie no good," shouted Kokuba. He would have over balanced in his rage had he not steadied himself on one of his cronies. Then his eyes fastened on my moustache.

"Kempitana?" And out came his long sword.

"Blimey, he's going to cut it off" I said to myself, "and in his present state my head will go with it." Big as my moustache was I knew it did not present a large enough target for this drunken sot. I had often seen and heard Kokuba on his nightly sword slashing and thought I was to be the victim this time. He waved his long sword over my head. I could feel the draught of air as it whistled by. This is the end, I thought, there is nothing to stop him, and nothing will be said afterwards. He's the chief Nip here. But after a minute or two of this he said "Kempie okay," kicked me in the backside and Bill and I returned to the Police hut. We felt we were justified in saying, "A policeman's lot is not a happy one."

One of the detestable jobs MP's had to do was to catch men who had broken camp when they returned with booty. All this was confiscated, but what happened to it? Was the hooch poured away and the rest of the stuff sent to the hospital? I have often thought since, that a fair amount found its way to far less deserving places. I remember one fellow being caught by a Nip on returning to camp. He was loaded with tomatoes and instead of beating or arresting him the Nip made him eat them all on the spot. It reminded me of the occasion when a Nip guard found one of our chaps smoking at work, and punished him by making him smoke ten cigarettes at once.

I didn't like the way some of the police sneaked round the huts in Jap Happies, eavesdropping. They would find out who intended to break out at night and where they were going. This meant that the rest of us would break out too, and wait for them in some forlorn jungle track. It was all very well to wait for men who were disposing of stolen kit or quinine in the Kampongs, but who the hell wanted to wait three or four hours, outside the camp fence, bitten by mosquitoes and then run the risk of being shot by a Nip on the way back. All this to catch one of our own men who was trying to get something extra for himself and his pals. One night I was returning from such an exploit and attempting to enter camp on my own. I reached the fence and was about to sneak through, when lucky for me, a Nip several feet away succumbed to one of their terrible habits, he drew up his guts to spit. I dropped where I was and lay in the wet mud for what seemed like hours until it was safe for me to climb through the fence.

In September the floods came again and they were worse than those we experienced two years previously in 1942. This time POW's and Nips worked side by side to stem the flow of water. Thais came through the camp in boats, and whenever a Nip went downstream he wore a lifejacket. There was the same trouble with flooded bed platforms, lost kit and insanitary conditions. Boats were loaded at a point opposite our police hut and one day, a Nip bawled, "English Soldier," to a big fellow working on a boat. He was ordered to carry a Nip Sergeant Major through the swirling muddy water to the Pom Pom. The Nip was dressed up in his finest – he was probably off to the nearest brothel – and he climbed on the man's back, like the character in "Sinbad the Sailor". All went well for a time and then the bearer's feet slipped and making certain he grabbed the Nip's legs tightly, they both disappeared under the water. The expression on the Nip's face was a tonic to everybody. We howled with laughter as did the Nip officer who witnessed the scene, and the victim could only join in, instead of beating the unfortunate bearer.

This was perhaps the only really bright feature of my time as a policeman, I had become disillusioned and so towards the end of September 1944, was glad to find myself included in another party for "up country".

Chapter 19

Takunun and Bombing

*"I never saw sad men who looked
With such a wistful eye
Upon that little patch of blue
We prisoners called the sky."*

Oscar Wilde

It was now the Nips' practice to issue a limited amount of clothing to parties leaving Chungkai whatever their destination. We were no exception, our party was paraded in the afternoon, and the Nip quartermaster inspected to decide which men received the items he had made available. There were the now familiar "Bangkok Bowlers", a few pairs of canvas boots, some with a separate big toe, thin cotton pants of various colours and also a few vests. No man was allowed to receive more than one item, if he received a hat he could still be without footwear. Many men got nothing, I was fortunate to receive a pair of rubber boots, they were far too small but I cut pieces out of the heels and toes to make them fit. The same evening we paraded again with our kit ready to leave, we were counted and searched and our hut searched too. It would mean a beating to be found possessing two articles of the same sort, but they were also looking for such things as razors, knives and pens etc. Our hiding places were usually effective and the Nip search revealed very little. They never thought, for example, of cutting the rice bread we had baked with forbidden articles hidden inside.

We were not looking forward to the journey. It was bound to be uncomfortable, we expected that, as the Nip transport arrangements were always bad. In addition, there was now the danger of bombing by Allied planes, which were over daily and naturally concentrating on the railway. We had heard that a number of trains had been bombed and machine gunned, killing many of our men. It was good to know that the fortunes of war could be turning in our favour. We didn't mind them attacking the Nips, but none of us were anxious to be killed by our own planes after surviving nearly three years as prisoners. The Nips seldom made advance arrangements for transporting their prisoners, or so it appeared to us, and we had to wait several hours by the track. When our train arrived, it was about what we expected – closed steel-sided vans like the ones that had brought us from Singapore. To make matters worse they were half full of cement. We crammed in the best we could and settled down among the sacks. A good start for some of the new kit! The guards had ordered, that because conditions were so cramped, the men should ride on the tops of the trucks. We all got inside!

The Nip train drivers were shocking amateurs and stopped the train every two or three kilometres, only to start again with much jolting and banging. Anybody on the truck tops would have certainly been thrown off. A speed of more than twenty miles an hour was not possible without de-railing the trucks. Such was the state of the "permanent way" we had built.

Passing over Wampo viaduct next morning was quite a thrill. It was built round the side of a cliff and had only been completed by POW's a few weeks before. If the men on this work had been anything like us, we knew there was certain to be the odd piece of deliberate shoddy workmanship. Who of us had expected to have to ride on the bloody railway, we thought it would only be Nips. We knew that it only needed one support to weaken, and the whole train would drop into the river many feet below.

Having got safely over at about two miles an hour, we were surprised to see how big Wampo station had become. There were several sets of lines, sidings and an engine repair shop. We received a meal here and were split into parties to do a few hours work, digging shelters, erecting camouflage and clearing a strip of jungle for another siding. We hadn't had any sleep but were glad of the opportunity to stretch our legs.

Later in the day we moved off again, an engine at each end of the train. Had we not been prisoners, travelling in great discomfort, we might have been enchanted by the wonderful scenery, but the cement sacks, and the fear of Allied bombings, crushed any desire

DEE

Wampo bridge or viaduct, another crude but effective construction round the side of a mountain, with the river flowing many feet below.

for sight seeing. But while we could ignore the scenery, and I suppose I did, it was impossible to ignore the Kanu viaduct. This was very high and constructed on several tiers of wooden supports. It was horseshoe in shape, and travelling in the centre of the train, it was possible to see both engines at once, and very nearly shake hands with the drivers. It was a comparatively long bridge, and being aware that some trucks had crashed down into the jungle from previous trains, we were mighty relieved to get over and settle down to our former apathy.

Brankassi station was reached after dark but we were not allowed to de-train owing to rat-plague. Several Nips, but no British had died from it. Who were the rats anyway? We were glad to get away from Bankassi which had become a frequent target for our bombers, and next morning a short journey brought us to Takanun, our destination.

After marching for a kilometre, along a narrow path through the jungle, we came to a clearing where Nips were erecting a hut. It turned out this was to be our sleeping quarters and was complete except for the bed platforms. This was something new. Never before had the Nips worked for us! The rest of the day was spent in cutting bamboo from the jungle, making bed platforms and digging latrines.

For a week we were employed on jungle clearing and hut building. The river flowed some seventy yards from the hut and we cut a path through to it, hewing rough steps down the steep banks. From here we obtained water for all purposes, but we also found it ideal for a swim when we had a day off. These Nips were quite a good lot, and worked side by side with us. This was their first contact with Prisoners of War and they had no idea of the treatment we had received from their compatriots. We took jolly good care to bring them up on the right lines. Their officer seemed quite a humane chap, it must be said that he did all he could to help us during our stay in his camp.

In the course of our jungle clearing we found the site of a previously used hut, and nearby uncovered the graves of nine POW's. We were a mixed bunch, Cambridgeshires, Norfolks, Suffolks and twenty Dutchmen, one of whom found the grave of his brother who, so he heard, had been beaten to death by the Nips. We cleaned up the area and put a fence round the graves, building the second hut on the other side. Unfortunately, the camp was alive with mosquitoes and many men went down with malaria. It was a particularly virulent kind producing terrible vomiting and left each sufferer very weak. We hadn't been there long before two men died and we buried them alongside the nine Dutchmen's graves. Our MO himself caught the disease but stoutly refused to be sent down country.

Life at Takanun was better than in most of our former camps, but the food was scanty, and of extremely poor quality. There was also a shortage of cooking utentsils. The Nip officer tried to get things improved but the rations were issued farther down the line, very little seemed to reach us and the Nips were living almost as badly as us.

The poor rations and lack of containers for cooking purposes, in a diverse way, provided us with a considerable amount of light relief. It was the usual practice, until they were moved to separate camps, for at least one British officer to accompany a party of men leaving a large base camp. He would be responsible for POW discipline and also see that we didn't get too raw a deal from the Nips. Our party had been no exception, and a Major Rogers was now in charge of our camp. Not a very tall man, he was always smartly dressed, as far as POW's were concerned, and full of self importance. God knows where he had been until now, but he still possessed a decent bush hat, shirt, shorts, socks, boots and putties. He was far better dressed than any Nip. Making sure that we paraded before him every few days, he would stand in front of us, his long moustache bristling, smart kit and self assurance, giving the air of being a Major General at the very least. His speech always followed the same pattern, we would know almost exactly what was coming word for word:

"I am on top of the world," he would say, "the news is excellent. Now I'll just put you in the picture," and there would follow an account of his attempts to extract stores from the Nips, concluding with the anti-climax, "and in the end I got two tubs and fifty candles, but no containers."

It doesn't require a lot of imagination to understand why he was known as "Top of the World Roger" to us.

We supplemented our scanty meals with pig weed and any odd green stuff from the jungle. It was a wonder we didn't poison ourselves. We managed to steal some "stink fish", a type of dried fish, from a nearby Nip store, and grilled it on a piece of tin. As the fish became hot the maggots started wriggling, but as someone remarked, "it all goes the same way home and they can't be worse than the snakes, dogs and cats we've eaten before!"

Our work was to maintain about five kilometres of track. The line ran through mountainous country and there were many wooden bridges in our sector, some over quite deep gulleys and ravines. For the first few weeks we had the job of repairing a stretch of line that had been flooded. Parts of the embankment were washed away, rails and sleepers had been disturbed and sections of track needed re-laying. At first we weren't worked terribly hard, by previous standards, but found the walk to and from sites quite exhausting, particularly because of the heavy gear that needed carrying.

Due to the many bends and, no doubt, faults in the line, trucks were always being derailed. We were frequently turned out during the night to clear the line. In our little Jap Happies we were perfect fodder for the thousands of mosquitoes which multiplied during the hours of darkness. By the most primitive methods and quite often sheer manpower, the trucks were put back on the line. When this proved impossible, we pulled or levered them from the track, tipped them over the embankment, to leave them dumped on the edge of the jungle.

The day after these emergencies was always spent in jacking up the rails, changing damaged sleepers, and generally making the line serviceable, until the next derailment, which usually didn't take long to occur.

One night a truck came off the rails and bounced along the track for over a kilometre, before the driver became aware of it. In the course of its run it passed over two bridges and shoved the sleepers along into groups of six or seven, like a pack of cards. We toiled most of the night, in pitch darkness, helped by the occasional use of a lantern, standing on cross pieces of timber, not more than a foot width, banging the sleepers back into some sort of order. As daylight came we realised that we had been working with the prospect of dropping sixty feet into the gorge below, had we made one false step! We finished the job on our hands and knees!

On one occasion several of us were unloading ballast off a truck which had been unhitched from the rest of the train. We shovelled away until someone shouted "We're moving". Some idiot had failed to apply the brake. The wagons gained speed. I thought of the state of those bends and uneven track. If I stayed on, where would I end? I made up my mind and jumped, hitting the side of the embankment with an undignified sprawl, rolling over several times before regaining my feet, but relieved to find I was still in one piece. Another chap who jumped broke his ankle but a couple remaining on came to no harm, after a hair raising run of a kilometre or so, the truck came to a halt on a level section of track.

Our free time in the evenings was spent round fires in the hut. Sometimes we had a sing-song, a general knowledge quiz or maybe a talk if someone fancied having a go. So far from interfering, the Nips seemed to sympathise with us and would come and join in. Two of them, Way No and Yamura, seemed to vie with each other to give us privileges, as far as this was possible in such circumstances. Sometimes they would let us break off work early, and tell us to Yasumi in the jungle, until it was time to return to camp. However, there had to be one black sheep in the fold, and he received the nicknames of "Goldrush" and "Deep Purple" from us. The former referred to his teeth, he had a mouthful of gold ones, and the latter to his complexion, and the tone of his voice. He was always ready to beat us, and keep us working very hard for extra long hours. All he ever said in a grunting like voice was "Speedo, Taxan Shigoto, Yasumi ni", which we understood to mean, "Work like hell, do plenty of it and no rest."

We had one day off in ten, when we did our little bits of washing, scrounged food, such as weeds from the jungle, and generally tried to improve our lot. The river being so close, we were able to swim, and with improvised tackle some chaps managed to catch a few fish.

Life continued like this until December. The same routine, repairs to the line, replacing sleepers and sometimes a length of rail. Very poor food, but not bad Nips. We had certainly experienced a lot worse. The steady work and moderate conditions of living made us think it might go on like this forever. Then came a sudden change. And it came out of a clear blue sky!

On the evening of the 8 December 1944, we were having our meal of rice and stew, when the heavy drone of planes was heard. "Charlie" the recci plane had been over each day, and there had been the odd plane at night. But this was something different. Nearer and nearer. Everybody forgot the food and rushed outside to see what was happening. Soon seven four engined bombers appeared and flew over our camp heading down country towards Brankassi. Several waves of seven bombers followed. This was the end, we thought. Freedom at last. We became excited and ran out into the open space waving our arms as the planes passed overhead.

Then it happened. Several bombers broke formation, turned and flew back over the camp. Bomb doors opened and down came the bombs. In no time we had scattered into the jungle, taking shelter wherever we thought it might be safe. Surely it wasn't to end like this? Nearly three years up to now, surviving all manner of hardships only to be killed by our own planes? We crouched in the jungle for over an hour, while bombing and machine gunning continued. It couldn't go on much longer, could it? There must be a limit to what these planes could carry? When we were able to give attention to other things than our own safety we listened to the bombing and machine-gunning going on elsewhere. Our planes were really making a "do" of it. Brankassi seemed to be getting its share, as were many other parts of the line. More than two hours elapsed, before all the bombers had flown back to base and we filtered back to our huts. There was only one topic of conversation, there could be little sleep, if any, that night. Something close to our camp had received quite a pounding, we wondered what the target had been. We soon found out. It was getting dark when the Nips ordered a party of us to work on the line.

When we got there it was practically dark and there was little to see, save that a train had been bombed in the cutting near the camp, and several Nips and POW's been killed. A roll call revealed five Dutchmen missing but it was too dark to do anything that night. The train had been split into two on arrival of the aircraft, the front half had escaped most of the damage so all the survivors boarded this section and the train moved off. It looked very much as though some of us would have plenty to do in the morning. The Nips took us back to camp.

Sleep certainly didn't come easily. There was too much to occupy the mind.

So the rumours we had heard must have had some truth in them! And the Nips had been trying to convince us that India was in their hands, and Australia too. For a long time we'd been getting news of Allied successes in Europe. The Nips in the camp had talked to us about their homes, and mournfully told us that Japan had been bombed, and how they wished their country had kept out of the war. The trainloads of fighting Nips who had been carried up the line looked thoroughly fed up, and this lent colour to the rumour that all was not going well with them. And there'd been the civilian Nip in charge of the station, he was always quite decent to us and willing to talk. He said the Allies were bombing anywhere that Nips might be congregated and expressed the conviction we should soon be free.

Ever since we became prisoners, Christmas was a target date for freedom, even in the early days of 1942 it was "We will be free by Christmas", the same in 1943, dare we hope our target of Christmas 1944 was to be realised? Surely there wasn't enough time.

We received small snippets of news from Tamils working near us on another sector of line, but the most reliable "griff" seemed to come from a mysterious Thai trader known to us as Pong. Nobody that I had heard of had ever admitted seeing the man, yet everybody believed in his existence. He certainly brought the news and was pro British. I wondered if the big Thai in the spotless white top and black silk bell bottomed trousers was Pong. I had seen him in various camps selling goods to stores and canteens. But, whoever he was, the hopeful news he had been spreading received corroboration by the arrival of the bombers.

The following morning we were up earlier than usual and after swallowing our "pap", watery tasteless jam, and a mug of hot water, we paraded for roll call and work. Thirty of us were selected for a special job and were supplied with picks, shovels and ropes. We asked the Nip what we were going to do. He could only make signs indicating places and bombs and from his gestures, we thought he wanted us to recover unexploded bombs. We had no intention of doing this, and told him so, when we suddenly realised that our task was to find the bodies of the five missing Dutchmen. The scene of the bombing by daylight revealed what a good job the bombers had done. One engine and several steel covered trucks had been completely wrecked and the rest of the train was riddled with bullets. And this in spite of being sheltered by a bank on either side of the train, with mountains above it. The blast had torn down trees and several acres of jungle were completely flat. We searched sometime without success until a shout told us that someone had found something. It was a blackened charred arm and hand. Concentrating our search in this area, we found other odd parts until we had a near complete body which we buried in a nearby bomb crater. Our grisly search continued all morning and by early afternoon we had accounted for and buried the remains of another three men. We continued to search and had almost abandoned all hope of finding the fifth when we found his body, completely unmarked in thick undergrowth some yards into the undisturbed jungle. He had either been killed by the blast or perhaps suffered a heart attack.

After the men had been buried, we were careful to mark their graves with large wooden crosses, in the hope that our planes might see them and realise that prisoners were in the area. The Nips marked their graves with single up-right posts. After the burial a Dutchman offered prayers and we all, Nips included, stood with bowed and bared heads.

We thought the bombing might produce an outbreak of Nip brutality by way of revenge, but it didn't. The Nips were really scared, but oddly enough, seemed pleased with the turn events had taken. They fenced us in after the first day of bombing and put us on trench digging and making shelters. When we worked on the line one of us was appointed spotter to signal the approach of Allied aircraft. We spent more than two days camouflaging the siding, various parts of the line and huts, using bamboo and all manner of growth from the jungle. Following that first attack the bombers returned the following night and continued to do so for weeks. They usually came over about the time of our evening meal, and we got accustomed to getting our food and taking it undercover to eat. We all became very excited and rather nervous, but it soon became clear that the planes made for big stations, trains and engines. News reached us that Tamarkan bridge had been bombed and many prisoners killed and wounded. There were so many rumours circulating that we didn't know what to believe. We heard that Allied troops had landed nearby and with all the aerial activity it certainly seemed probable. Our British camp commandant "On top of the world" Rogers told us everything appeared to be going well, we must keep our heads and if a chance came make the most of it. What discussions we had, and the plans we made, that were never put into action.

We heard rumours that all prisoners were to be sent down country and this was taken as a good sign. Sure enough several train loads of prisoners passed on their way down and the camps on either side of us were vacated. We felt it would be safer if we stayed where we were for the time, and it looked as though we would, when we were given the job of loading a whole Nip camp, several kilometres away, for down country. Things were beginning to move fast.

Just before Christmas we received orders to pack all the Nips' kit, tools and equipment, load it onto a train and be ready to leave ourselves the next day for Tamarkan. We didn't like the idea of this. Tamarkan was too near the steel bridge where several of our pals had been killed. The prospect of the train journey wasn't too pleasant either. Trains were regular targets and our planes' success rate was becoming quite impressive. But we had to go, and early next morning we were on our way once more. The Nips were sorry to see us go and, in a sense, we were sorry to leave them. They were the best we had come up against so far, they had treated us well, and it wasn't likely that the next lot would be so considerate.

We drew into Brankassi just after daylight and after waiting several hours, were moved into the jungle, some three hundred yards from the station where we were told to wait until dark. The

Nips moved mainly by night now, because daylight bombing had accounted for so many of their engines. I saw five completely out of action in Brankassi station and heard that in the first big air raid as many as twenty five were crippled over two hundred kilometres of line. The day passed quietly, we laid down and rested in the shade. The area was crammed with Nip fighting troops doing the same, while waiting to resume their journey to the fighting in Burma. At least that's where we thought they were going, in spite of some of the Nips telling us that they had taken India. Just after dark we boarded the train and although we expected air attack at any moment, it never came. We had an uneventful journey as far as Wun Lun, which we reached at noon the next day. Here we had to leave the train and scatter into the jungle. A single plane flew about for some time while the train was split into sections and camouflaged. After dark we were on the move again and an hour or so later reached Tamarkan station.

Chapter 20

Another Christmas

"I have but one merit, that of never despairing"
                                                Marshal Foch

So here I was, once more back in Tamarkan camp. Perhaps it wouldn't be long before I'd be back in England! Inside the camp we paraded again to be counted. Cold, tired and hungry, the drink of hot, sweet burnt rice coffee was very acceptable. This was a good start as we hadn't tasted sugar for a long time, but it was about the only item on the credit side of the ledger. We were put into a tumble down hut for the night, and groping about in the dark, flopped down to sleep where we could. In the morning we saw that the hut had been nearly blown down in the bombing, and must have been used as a place for dumping rubbish. By this time we were used to any conditions and took a philosophical view on life that things could always be worse. At least we were still alive not like so many of our colleagues who would never return home.

Everybody in Tamarkan was air raid conscious, and with very good reason considering what had already happened, and the camp's nearness to the important steel bridge. The Nips were scared stiff, and sounded the alarm when planes were miles away or just a recci plane overhead. During our first day there were several warnings and we had to hurry to trenches that had been dug in the shade of banana trees. Our officers told us not to panic at the alarm but go quietly to the trenches, however the Nips had other ideas and hurried us to cover with screams and blows. On the sounding of the alarm they rushed all over the camp, complete with steel helmets and fixed bayonets, ready to give a prod of encouragement to any slow moving prisoner. The number of guards was doubled and they took up positions to ensure that no one escaped.

Tension was high in the camp, a man scrambling hurriedly off his bed platform for the latrines at night, could start a frenzied rush to the trenches. Every visit of Allied planes found us midway between fear of being killed by our own men and the pleasure at the thought of our side being so much on the offensive. "Charlie" the recci plane had been over most days and continued to do so during our stay, in fact his visits were so regular that if he failed to appear there would be much discussion as to the reason why.

Our main work was to dig a large ditch three metres deep and four wide, round the camp. The displaced earth was deposited on the outside of the ditch, to form a steep bank two metres high, a bund with a path several metres wide on which the guards could patrol. The bund appeared to serve several purposes, it was to keep us in and the natives out, and at the same time indicate to Allied planes that the place was a POW camp. Because of the way events were supposed to be shaping, it was now forbidden to contact or speak to a native, to be caught attempting to do so would bring severe punishment to both parties concerned. Discipline was very strict, the Nips were a far different bunch to those we had left up country.

A Nip bugle call would summon us to roll call night and morning. We paraded in working battalions, all mixed units, in files of five or ten and numbered in the now familiar Japanese language. The officer in charge had to declare in Japanese, how many of his men were on parade, how many sick in hospital and in huts. The numbers were never taken for granted now, the Nips would take ages trying to reconcile the figures, counting the men on parade themselves while their colleagues counted the sick elsewhere. It was nothing to stand an hour as the pantomime progressed. The Nips invariably scratched the numbers in the dust at their feet, removing little jockey type hats, rubbing their shaven heads in bewilderment, as their little sums failed to add up as required. But one of our officers had a different method which made things even more confused, he would draw figures in the air as though writing on a blackboard. It was real entertainment to watch him put several lots of figures on the imaginary board, draw a line and make a total. If a mistake occurred, he would pretend to rub the figure out and start again, while the Nips watched in mystified amazement. In the ranks we would watch all this and say, "There he goes at his dumb charades again". Eventually another Nip bugle call would indicate that we could fall out.

The Nip Camp Commandant was nicknamed Bluebeard, on

account of his appearance, rather than by reason of any known tendency to uxorcide. He was short, and had an enormous black beard, through which one caught occasional glimpses of gold teeth. He was always smartly dressed in white shirt, shorts and socks. His own men were afraid of him. He was frequently ordering them to be beaten, but to us he was fair and just.

The food was very poor and inadequate, as rice formed the bulk of our diet we felt the immediate effect, should the amount issued be reduced. This was the case at Tamarkan. In the jungle, on our last party, we received just over a pint of cooked rice per meal. This had not been enough, but here the ration was less than a pint, and on average a quarter pint of stew. We were always hungry.

It was extremely cold at nights in our dilapidated huts. Very few men in my battalion still had a blanket, and those still being used were threadbare and covered in patches of sacking. My own list of kit would be a fair sample of the average POW's possessions at this particular time, some even might be lucky and have a little more, but there would be others with far less. I still had the canvas boots issued when I went to Takanun, too small and now practically worn out. An old PT vest and a pair of blue cotton shorts, gaily patched with pieces of rag. A "Jap Happy", a groundsheet in three pieces, stiff like roofing felt through constant use. A messtin and a broken spoon with make-shift bamboo handle. An ex-milk tin complete with wire handle which was now my drinking mug. Two rice sacks, one which served as a blanket, the other being used as a shirt. Possibly the most important item, an old army water bottle, which I took nearly everywhere to prevent it being pinched. I had a Japanese type mat to sleep on, complete with a copious colony of bugs.

I used my Jap Happy for work, shorts and vest for "special occasions" and if able to get into the river would be naked and hopefully dry in the sun. Very few men had towels, and I hadn't seen any soap for months.

Our third Christmas 1944, as prisoners, was spent very much like the former two. We awoke Christmas morning, and it was just like the start of a normal day except that we weren't harassed, and had all been given the day off. We were also expecting to receive some better meals, but the breakfast of rice and boiled soya beans didn't do much to raise our hopes. During the morning some of the "resident" POW's put on a pantomine, "Aladdin", it was quite a good show, in spite of the make shift scenery and the improvised props and costumes. The Dutch Eurasion playing the part of the princess was excellent and it was hard to realise that this "lovely girl" was a man! Good God! How long had it been since we'd seen a real live white girl?

Our Christmas dinner consisted almost entirely of vegetables which must have been saved for the occasion. We even had a small piece of boiled meat. For "sweet" we were given "Christmas Pudding". Hardly the real thing, it was made entirely from rice and gula sugar. We finished with a mug of sweet tea.

In the afternoon we crowded round to watch the Christmas Football International, Britain v Holland. All the camp appeared to be there, the crowd round the rough earth pitch must have been seven or eight men deep. The match was interrupted dramatically by the sound of an approaching plane. Spectators vanished like smoke, including the Nips, but it turned out to be one of theirs, taking the chance that Christmas offered, of flying without danger from our chaps. The evening meal was similar to that served up midday except it was followed by "Christmas Cake" instead of the pudding. Made entirely from rice again it was the best dufor I ever tasted as a POW.

That night, with stomachs feeling comfortably full for the first time in months, we sat around in the dark discussing the likelihood of our being free by the following Christmas. Surely the Allies must attack soon, before the Monsoon came. If they didn't we should be in Thailand another year, or perhaps forever! It didn't bear thinking about!

Two days after Christmas excitement ran high again as all work on the "Bund" was stopped. Rumour said the camp was to be abandoned, as it was too near the steel bridge, and it proved to be true. A hundred men were formed into an advance party, and I was pleased to find myself included, I would be glad to get away from this place. We paraded just after daylight the following day and in addition to our meagre kit we were given equipment and tools to carry for the Nips. We were to march to Chungkai along the railway track and be prepared to do a hard days work on arrival.

Chapter 21

Chungkai Again

"The most anxious man in a prison is the governor."
George Bernard Shaw

The short march was uneventful, we arrived at Chungkai mid morning and were immediately paraded for general check and search. Whenever we left or arrived at a camp searches invariably followed the same sort of pattern, this is typical of what normally took place. We formed into four ranks, well spaced out and laid all our belongings out on the ground in front of us. We then formed up again, a few yards to the rear of the area, now strewn with all manner of junk. Several Nips came along and turned over our miserable belongings, occasionally picking out something they thought we shouldn't keep, but there was seldom anything of any importance for them to find. On the back of an old envelope in my kit was a rough sketch of one of my pal's home district in England and the Nips pounced on this, thinking possibly, that it could be a plan of escape.

After all our kit had been examined, it was our turn to be individually searched before being allowed to return to our places. When we arrived there were only about two hundred men in Chungkai, and most of them turned out to watch the proceedings from a safe distance. We recognised many of them as belonging to the "Same old faces". Men who, one way or another, had managed to dodge all the up country working parties, down country too for that matter, and have a comparatively easy time as prisoners.

We started work immediately, re-building dilapidated huts in order to accommodate the thousands of men that were to follow. Daily more and more men arrived from Tamarkan, the so called fit were being sent first and on arrival joined in the hut building. As the numbers of POW's and Nips increased so the discipline tightened. Numbers were constantly checked and a POW night picquet was positioned in every hut. We took it in turns, an hour each, and our period of duties came round about every third night. It meant standing at the end of the hut with wooden tallies, one of which had to be taken by every man leaving the hut to answer the call of nature. Woe betide anyone found outside a hut without one. The number of men in each hut was displayed on a board outside, and at least twice nightly several Nips would descend on the huts, and count the prostrate bodies. The man on duty had to report, in Japanese, to each Inspecting Nip, the numbers involved and the whereabouts of those not in the hut. Should his numbers not tally or the Nip be in a bad mood, the certain result was a bashing. The same treatment was metered out if the man on duty was caught sitting down. It paid to keep awake, remain standing and, most important, learn enough of the language to pass on the information demanded. In addition to the nightly checks, the Nips were for ever searching our kit for illicit articles, but seldom found anything. All knives, pencils etc, were buried in the ground or hidden in hollow bamboo.

The Nip Colonel in charge at Chungkai was Ishi – to us he appeared fat, old and with a deadly smile. He could speak no word of English, and all his orders were given to us through an interpreter who resembled a turtle and was known to us as "Turtle Neck". He was a nasty specimen and we often wondered whose orders we received, were they his or Ishi's? He turned up at one of our concerts, went on stage and bashed the performers. They were doing a sketch in which Tarzan swung onto the stage, at the end of a rope, and rescued a maiden from the clutches of an ape, who did look amazingly like one of our captors. Turtle Neck demanded that the show end immediately. It did, and within a few days, the stage had been pulled down too. Later on, I remember at another concert, this sketch was put on again, and one of our chaps dressed as Turtle Neck, repeated his act on the stage. It took us all in at first, until the imitation Turtle Neck was thrown bodily into the audience, by the other members of the cast.

When the hut building was completed we were put on the job of building a huge "bund" round this camp. A party of officers cleared an area of jungle in preparation and the rest of us, under the supervision of warrant officers, did the digging. It was back to task work again. We were formed into parties of twenty five and allocated a strip of land to dig out and complete in seven days, if we completed the task in less, the rest of the time could be Yasumi. We had seen all this before, no way did we intend getting caught out again. We programmed our work to finish just inside the time allowed. The Nips in charge of the work were anxious to have a few hours off themselves, and as they were more reasonable than some we had come across before, a satisfactory arrangement was unofficially agreed. They wouldn't harass us, or increase our task, in return we would finish in time for us all to have a half day off.

When the camp was encircled, three bridges for access were built and a start made on another bund down the centre to divide off the Nip area from ours. "Charlie" the recci plane came over everyday, he seemed to hover unchallenged, high over the camp for hours. He would have had no difficulty in seeing what we were doing and known that we were POW's. Five hundred or so near naked men, sweat streaming off our brown skinny bodies, we must have looked like a swarm of ants, as we toiled in the blazing sun.

The food in Chungkai was really bad, and insufficient to sustain us, breakfast was a piece of bread, three inches long, one and a half wide and about an inch thick. We called it bread, it was made from rice and ground soya beans, when baked it had the texture of a piece of wood. With this we received a spoonful of "jam", a tasteless concoction made from pumpkin and pomelo skins. The other two meals were the usual rice and stew, little of it and very poor quality rice, full of husks, weevils and rat dung. We seldom saw a "dufor" as it appeared that cooking oil was almost unobtainable, in spite of the money stopped from our meagre pay for messing. What on earth would the food have been like without our contribution, heaven knows, and where was the money going?

Although the food was bad, the rumours and news were good and each day brought more hope of freedom. It was taken as a good sign when the officers were separated from us. Removed from our camp, that is. They had never been integrated with other ranks, always having their own separate area of quarters, they lived and fed apart from the men. I think the opinion we formed of a few of them, had been more than a little unjust. The odd one, here and there could certainly have done more to ease the plight of the ordinary prisoner, but no doubt most of them did their best. We were sorry to see them go. They were brought in from all camps up and down the line and put into a separate camp at Kanchanburi. At Chungkai we were left with several Medical Officers and a Padre. Camps would in future be administered by Warrant Officers.

General opinion was that this action indicated that the war could not be going in the Nips favour, surely our time would soon come. The Nips must be scared that the officers might be able to organise some large scale escape.

At night we would sit about in the dark, indulging in the luxury of talking of the day when we could exchange rice for roast beef and yorkshire pudding. The menus discussed were torturous on our near empty stomachs. Eggs, bacon and mushrooms for breakfast. Real bread, butter and marmalade. Tea with sugar and milk. New potatoes, green peas, carrots and all manner of English vegetables. What on earth did those things taste like? Then there were clothes; no longer would a Jap Happy constitute our entire clothing, every day alike. We'd have decent suits, a shirt and a tie and a good pair of shoes on our feet. A clean bed to sleep in, sheets and blankets too. No more laying on hard bamboo platforms full of bugs with a lice ridden sack for covering. No more centipedes, scorpions, ants or mosquitoes. There would be soap and hot water to bath in, also a clean towel on which to dry. Toothpaste, a brush and a comb and how about a mirror? Tell the time by a watch, instead of the stars or sun, and be free of the humiliation of being bullied and hectored by Nips.

The list was endless. Previously we had not dared to tantalize ourselves by mentioning such things as "tailor-made" cigarettes, glasses of beer, newspapers and women, but now the return to civilised life did not seem anything like so remote or impossible. Consequently, it came as a shock when yet another rumour proved to be true, another party was to go up into the dreaded jungle again, this time to an undisclosed destination. This dampened spirits a little, we were beginning to think the war was nearly over, surely we had been up country for the last time. Perhaps it would be the last time for the men being sent!

I found myself included in the party yet again, and with others, persuaded our Warrant Officer to go to the Nips and ask or demand an issue of clothing. He did his best but it wasn't enough, he obtained four pairs of canvas boots, three pairs of cotton shorts and six vests for the party of two hundred men. We had to manage the best we could and looked a sorry sight when we paraded for search before leaving. Most of us were barefooted, some had worn out boots, tied together with odd pieces of string or ties that were used for building, and the remainder wore home-made sandals or clogs.

Chapter 22

Beasts of Burden

"A few hours of mountain climbing turn a rascal and a saint into two pretty similar creatures. Fatigue is the shortest way to Equality and Fraternity – and, in the end, Liberty will surrender to sleep."
Friedrich Nietzsche
1844–1900

The customary search preceeded the usual uncomfortable journey, with the added sad reflection that, here I was, going up country again, when we all thought the war was as good as over and freedom just around the corner. We left Chungkai at night, sometime early in March 1945, with a British Sergeant Major in charge. In the early hours we reached Wampo, left the rail wagons and squatted by the track for well over an hour. After being counted numerous times, we were marched just over a kilometre through the jungle, until we came to the bank of the river where we were told to rest until dawn. All this was done without the Nips using lights, they were very wary of aerial attacks, although we neither saw nor heard planes in this operation. It was bitterly cold and the mosquitoes saw to it that we got no sleep, so we were not sorry when dawn came, and with it, two small boats tied together and handled by a young native. It took an hour to get us all across the river on this improvised ferry. Then we marched a short distance and found a small camp most effectively hidden in the jungle.

A Dutch interpreter appeared from one of the huts, said we were expected and told us a meal had been prepared. It had! Plain rice! Shortly other men came out of the huts, most of them Dutchmen, they were a sorry sight, thin, unshaven, broken in spirit, looking very ill and thoroughly depressed. There wasn't a fit man among them. Two Englishmen approached us, anxiously asking questions about life and conditions down country, and eagerly seeking news and rumours. They painted a very miserable picture of the life we were to expect on this side of the river. The rations, they told us, were terrible, nothing but plain rice to eat. There were no medical supplies or treatment, if you fell sick, you stayed sick. There was no chance of returning down country. The Nips were bastards and the work brutally hard, carrying rations for Nips many kilometres over mountainous country.

All this was confirmed immediately before we were able to finish our meal. We received a lecture from a Nip Sergeant Major, a typical bully, who managed to hit everybody during our short stay in this camp. He told us we had to move on further at once. We had twenty-two kilometres to march that day over rough and dangerous country. He warned us to keep close together because the area was infested with marauding tigers. Plain cooked rice was given us for the journey and we filled our water bottles. Some men still had the army issue type with webbing holders, others ordinary glass bottles with home made string carriers while some relied on hollow bamboo. In addition to our belongings, and the party's gear, we carried cooking utensils and dry rations for use at the next camp.

The march was all it promised to be, the road, or single track, was very rough and took us over a mountain during the first stage of the journey. The sun blazed down, and dust choked up our parched throats. We only dare take occasional sips of water, because we had no idea where the next supply would come from, or how long we would have to wait for it. I was thankful for my old Sergeant Major's army training and discipline here.

At midday, weary and almost out on our feet, we arrived at the next camp, Chilli Valley. There were only two small huts here and the sole occupants were five Nips and two Englishmen. This small camp was at the foot of another mountain, and we stayed long enough to eat the cold rice we had brought with us, and obtain information from the two resident POW's, as to what work we were expected to do.

The meal finished, we were off again, starting with a stiff climb, up a zig-zag path which had been cut in the mountain, up one side and down the other. We continued for about twenty kilometres and began to wonder how much further we were expected to go, or in fact were able to go. Most of us were completely exhausted, dragging one foot in front of the other, like worn out battery operated robots. We hadn't seen another human since leaving Chilli Valley. It was getting dark, when at last we passed through a banana plantation and came to a small Kampong, with an old Thai school in the middle of the clearing.

This was Bondei, our destination, and the place where we were to spend the night. From among the banana trees, several Dutchmen emerged with drums of boiled water, and we thankfully quenched our thirst. About one hundred Dutchmen were camped here, they had prepared a meal of plain rice and a little dried fish for us. This we quickly devoured and fell asleep from exhaustion, pretty well where we were.

We had been led to expect that we should move on next morning but found that plans had been changed over·night. After eating our plain rice breakfast the Nips said that work was waiting for us here at Bondei. All men were required immediately, a few remained in camp to clear a small area in which we would camp, and the others had to be ready to march. We were divided into pairs, each pair being given a bamboo pole about three inches in diameter and eight feet long. In amongst the banana trees were sacks of rice, large skips of vegetables such as pumpkin and sweet potatoes, tubs of a vitamin food called Misa and sometimes a skip of eggs. These items were slung on the poles, making loads of one hundred pounds or more. Shouldering the poles between us we set off, following a winding path up the mountainside in the opposite direction from which we had entered camp the day before. We carried our loads about five or six kilometres, climbing most of the time on a rough and narrow zig-zag path. It took all of four hours to reach our objective, a rendezvous point some little way over the Burma border, where Dutch prisoners met us and took over our loads.

We had been allowed three short rests on the way up but the whole exercise was a terrible strain, some of the weaker men found it impossible to manage their quota, but it had to be done, so unfortunately resulted in bigger loads for the rest of the party. The Dutchmen had come from a camp further on, they had been carrying Nips on improvised bamboo stretches and it didn't need much imagination to guess what our return loads would be. We saw to it they had a rough ride.

"Come on, shake the bastard up," we would shout to each other. This relieved our feelings and of course, meant nothing to the men we were carrying. That is except on one occasion, when the Nip passenger hopped off the stretcher as we reached Bondei and said in a strong American accent:

"Thanks fellows. The ride was swell but your language stinks!"

Our feet were in bad shape when we arrived at Bondei the day before, but now they were very much worse, blistered and bleeding, what would they be like tomorrow, when we had to do the same all over again?

Our kits had been moved and we found that our party had been allocated a small area round an old Thai building. No accommodation had been provided for us, or anything to use for building. The first few nights we slept on the ground anywhere we could. Later we improvised shelters from banana leaves, on bamboo frames, and slept under them. These were useless against tropical thunderstorms, and when there was heavy rain we sat or lay in the mud all night, with a great deal of singing to keep our spirits up. However wet it had been during the night, the hot sun dried us and our kit the next day.

Bondei was twenty or so kilometres west of Wampo and the railway and surrounded by mountains. Originally a Kampong, one or two deserted buildings were occupied by the Nips. Like many other buildings in the area, they were sited on poles about six feet from the ground and entered by means of a bamboo ladder. One small building became accommodation for our MO, the RSM in charge of our party, and shelter for anyone sick.

A small spring ran through the centre of the Kampong, this was our only water supply, we used it for everything, that used for drinking was always boiled. The food was appalling, nearly always plain rice with sometimes a small piece of dried fish, or perhaps some pumpkin water. The meal we took with us to eat at midday, was always cold and often gone sour. We supplemented our rations by collecting bamboo shoots, wild spinach, pig weed or anything from the jungle that we hoped was edible. We cooked the stuff on little individual fires in the evening, mixing it with anything we had managed to pinch from the Nip's rations during the day.

I used to try and become the rear half of a couple carrying a skip of eggs. After sharing the contents of my water bottle with my front half, I would pinch the eggs as we went along, and blow their contents into my bottle, adopting the method used with bird's eggs, when I was a boy. The result would be a welcome omelette or scrambled eggs on return to camp. Dried fish we hid in our Jap Happies, not the best of places perhaps, but the Nips didn't normally check there. They were always on the look out for thieving and to be caught would result in a beating, but it was always worth taking the risk. We stole cucumbers to suck out the

DEE

Beasts of burden.

juice, losing so much perspiration we were becoming very near dehydrated. Leaves from lime trees we boiled in water, and drank five or six pints of the brew each evening, always being careful to fill our bottles for the next days march.

Despite our blisters and bleeding feet, chronic diarrhoea and various other complaints, work continued daily in very much the same way. Small parties of men were camped at intervals along this track, which had been made from Wampo to Tavoy. Rations and other supplies were being brought up by train to Wampo Station, ferried over the river, and from there onwards manhandled by the POW's, using little handcarts where possible from Chilli Valley as far as Bondei. At Bondei we acted as a staging post, working in both directions, we collected supplies to go further westwards up the road towards Tavoy, and after transferring them, collected other items to go down. I did hear that other forms of transport had been tried, small pack horses and even cattle. They hadn't proved to be very satisfactory, the Nips found that we made better beasts of burden, and no doubt we were a lot cheaper to feed too.

During all this time we had heard rumours of tremendous air activity on the part of the Allies. We knew some of this must be true, because planes frequently passed over our camp, and we often heard bombing in the distance. Wampo was bombed on several occasions, and news reached us that the bridge had been destroyed and the station severely damaged. We understood there had been both POW and Nip casualties. We frequently had to take what cover we could when carrying our loads, and the Nips were scared planes would bomb our camp. Men now unfit for the slave labour, were made to camouflage the place. The old Thai school was covered with palms, and the open space surrounding it planted with almost full grown banana trees.

To add to the Nip's problems, and to a certain extent ours, detection of tigers' spoor a couple of hundred yards from the camp caused great excitement. Two days later, when further evidence of their existence was found no more than twenty yards from our latrines, everyone became generally worried. One or more must have been prowling very near as we slept unprotected in the open. The Nips ordered that a number of fires be kept burning all night, at various points round the camp to frighten them away. It became our duty, taking one hour each, to keep the fires burning, and also extinguish them quickly when a Nip screamed "Skwarki", meaning aircraft.

The Nips at Bondei were amongst the worst I met, and that about sums up what the food was like too. Perhaps they were beginning to realise that all was not well, and the now almost daily appearance of Allied planes, must have confirmed their worst fears. The food was just about enough to keep us alive, but the quality so poor that we were rapidly becoming thin and emaciated. No doubt the Nips were being bullied to get more work done, and having less "fit" men to do it inflicted more bashings on those of us still struggling to work.

One day on our return journey from the mountain, we brought down a number of Dutch POW's and a few British, all sick, they had come from a camp further up the road to Tavoy. Seventy five per cent of them were being carried on improvised stretches. We took them back to our camp. They were in a pitiable state, all ill and dejected, completely worn out and about ready to give up the ghost. Little did we realise that within a few weeks, many of our party would look the same.

They told us that all POW's were being withdrawn from the road, only two parties remained above us, and they would be down in the next few days.

Shortly after this, the number of men employed on ration carrying was reduced, and the parties above us returned and made their way down to Chilli Valley, Wampo and, we presumed, down country, as had the party of sick men before them. Atap came up to us in place of rations, and our type of work changed dramatically. Some men cut bamboo from the nearby jungle, while others built dozens of small huts round the camp area, several hundred yards apart, and completely hidden in the jungle. They would have been invisible from the air, in fact we had considerable difficulty in locating some of them ourselves. More rations of the non-perishable type were sent up, and all this we stacked in the little shelters.

As this went on, we were made to dig hundreds of small fox holes. Other men collected, what must have amounted to, tons of old bamboo for firewood, stacking the stuff in neat piles all over the place. It would take months for a cookhouse to burn all that fuel and what about all the rations and fox holes? It seemed obvious to us what was planned. The Nips must be preparing a line of retreat. There was enough food, wood for cooking and shelters for thousands of them, several hundred at a time, if and when their orders came to clear out.

Our work at Bondei was now complete, and arrangements were made for us to go down country once again. The sick men were to make up the first party and the rest would follow in a few days. I was included in the number of sick. I was far from being fit, but my main problem was my right knee, it had become almost useless as a result of the strenuous marches. Many were suffering from far more serious complaints, such as dysentery, malaria and nearly all of us to some degree, malnutrition and beri beri. Sick though we were, we marched, or rather hobbled and staggered back to Wampo with only one short break at Chilli Valley. Here we ate the meagre meal that we'd brought with us from Bondei, plain rice and a piece of dried fish about the size of a man's little finger.

Chapter 23

Wampo

"The courage we desire and prize is not the courage to die decently, but to live manfully."
                                                    Thomas Carlyle

Wampo hospital camp was not more than a hundred yards in diameter, enclosed by a bamboo fence, and contained five small atap huts and a few tents. It was well hidden in the jungle on top of the river bank. We arrived just after dark and after being subjected to the usual number of checks, we were told to sit and await further instructions. This was the usual procedure, no one ever seemed to know exactly where we were supposed to go, or what to do with us, and it was always much worse for a party of sick.

After about an hour a British MO and a Dutch interpreter appeared, and together they sorted us out according to our various diseases. With another man I was sent to a hut housing semi-sick men, according to POW standards. The place was already overcrowded, and we were allocated a bed space of less than three feet by six feet between us, and a generous colony of bugs and lice to go with it.

Nearly all the men in the place were depressed and anxiously waiting to be sent down country, and the prospect of receiving some sort of treatment. When we arrived there were about three hundred occupying the place. The food was even worse than Bondei, and that was saying something, very short and absolutely tasteless. Breakfast was "pap", the watery plain boiled rice, the other two meals were rice and pumpkin water, no salt or any flavouring whatsoever.

The Nip Sergeant Major, in charge, was the same creature we had encountered when we passed through Wampo several weeks earlier, on our way up to Bondei. He was a terror, he hated the British, especially the sick ones, and did all he could to make things uncomfortable for us. There was a camp of so called fit men nearby, but we were not allowed to converse with them, should any of them come near our fence. In fact we were not allowed to move out of our huts unless it was absolutely necessary. He would swagger quietly through the camp and expect to be treated as if he were king. Any sick man failing to salute him would receive a bashing from the bamboo stick he always carried, day and night. He expected to be addressed as "Hancho" meaning Master. I didn't hear him receive this compliment from the British, although he was addressed in this manner by some of the Dutchmen and it made me squirm everytime I heard it. However, perhaps they were the wiser, at least it prevented them getting bashed.

The men in our hut being classed as light workers, were liable to be called out at anytime for fatigues. We dug air raid shelters, and carried heavy sacks of rice. This was light work according to the Nips, we received no pay for it whereas the workers on the outside parties were now receiving twenty five cents a day. Many men asked to be classed as fit, and join the parties outside where the conditions appeared to be better, and the money might buy that little extra to supplement the diet. It was not to be, all occupants of the sick camp had to remain until it was decided to send them down country.

At Bondei and Chilli Valley we had been warned to beware of tigers, here in Wampo, the largest animals to come to my notice were the far more friendly gibbons. The occasional one or two could be seen playing in the bushes, but in the early mornings they were often heard, hooting and making happy whistling sounds in the hills around. The story was often told of a POW squatting on a latrine at night in the dark, attempting to hold a conversation with the body occupying the space beside him. Finding it hard going and not receiving any replies, he put out his hand to see if the other chap was all right. On feeling a very hairy arm, and hearing a not quite human grunt, he beat a hasty retreat back to the hut, leaving behind his Jap Happy!

Air raids were frequent, the bridge and the station bombed. Allied planes often appeared without warning, and we would drop flat on our faces wherever we were. Other times we would crowd into several small trenches as the planes circled unhindered above. We couldn't help thinking what the result would be if they decided to bomb our camp, one dropped inside the boundary fence would have probably accounted for most of us. However, there were no Nip planes or anti- aircraft guns to drive them off, so the bombing was accurate and we did not suffer, in spite of being able to watch the bombs as they hurtled toward the bridge. We could even read the numbers on the planes, they were so low.

We all wanted to get away from this camp, and move down country where we thought the food and conditions would be better. If we were eventually going to Chungkai, as rumoured, we should be much safer too, it was one of the oldest POW camps in Thailand, and the Allies must be well aware of its existence.

While we were very anxious to leave Wampo, we could not help speculating as to what would happen to us, should the bombers choose the day of our move for another attack on the line. I suppose there were other targets worthy of attention in Thailand, but the railway, bridges and rolling stock, were targets most days and we didn't relish the idea of being part of that scene.

Just over a week had been spent in this camp, when orders were issued that all men originating from Number Two Group would be moving to Chungkai the following day, provided Allied aircraft allowed it. Men belonging to number four group would be following in a few days.

The Nips kept us in the camp until the following afternoon before deciding that it would be safe to move. Bombing usually started about eleven thirty in the morning, nothing had happened today and we only hoped they hadn't changed their routine. We moved down to the river where we waited to be ferried across in small groups. This was it. The journey of, "I wonder if they'll come today," had begun.

Just over a hundred of us were going to Chungkai and it took some time to get us all over the river. As each group reached the other side, they waited in the jungle until the whole crossing was completed. We were now ready to move off, and before we went, the Nip in charge explained to us, in his pidgin English, what he hoped to achieve. We were to march down the line to Arro Hill, a distance of approximately six kilometres, during the march he wanted us to hurry as much as possible, as he was most anxious not to be trapped alongside the railway, especially near Wampo bridge. In a mixture of Japanese, Dutch and English he insisted that we must, "speedo, in case Churchill sends the Skwarkies over."

The march of several kilometres to the edge of the bridge was uneventful. We waited in the jungle, to enable the stragglers to catch up and give everyone a rest, before attempting, what was most likely to be, the hardest part of the journey.

As I mentioned before, the bridge was built round a cliff face, with the river many feet below. Sections of the bridge had been destroyed, and gangs of POW's and Tamils were working with Nips to replace the damaged structures. The distance from one end to the other end of the bridge area, was well over two hundred yards, and it took an hour to get all our party to the other side. We clambered over debris and boulders up on the cliff face, and in places had to go down to the waters edge and up again. Our bombers had been accurate and efficient.

On reaching the other side, we were allowed in the jungle to Yasumi, fires were lit and we boiled water from the river to drink. We certainly needed it.

We also had the chance to talk to fellow prisoners who were replacing parts of the broken bridge. They said, it was being bombed and knocked down as fast as they could repair it. They told us that so far none of them had been injured in the bridge raids, though one party of men had a narrow escape one day, when the alarm was not given in time for them to get into the jungle, and they had to take refuge in a shelter on the cliff face.

Looking back at the bridge, I had time to reflect, and think how amazing it was that such a flimsy structure had been capable of taking the weight of steam engines, however slowly they limped across. The crazy wooden bridge was, or had been, just two long baulks of timber. These were made up of a number of trees, hewn to a more or less uniform size of about a foot square. Over these crude baulks the sleepers and lines had been laid. The primitive construction was supported on a complicated network of cross pieces, and the whole lot appeared to be clinging precariously to the cliff face, with the river rushing over the rocks below, hungrily waiting to engulf anything or anybody that fell. This was typical of the bridges we had built for our masters, it was a hair-raising experience to pass over them in a train, expecting the whole thing to collapse at anytime. It was, perhaps more frightening to pass over on foot, no safety rails, just an expanse of emptiness below, as we gingerly stepped from sleeper to sleeper, each one seemingly placed rather too far apart for comfort.

The Yasumi over, we continued along the railway track to Arro Hill, relieved to have left Wampo behind us. Everywhere there was evidence of air attacks. The bombers had done a good job.

At Arro Hill we had to wait in the jungle yet again. We stayed there until well after dark. It was nearly midnight when a train arrived. It continued onwards to unload its cargo at the edge of Wampo bridge, before returning to pick us up. The engine was a broken down wreck and showed how poorly off the Nips were for rolling stock. The journey was very slow, at times we had to stop and allow the engine to get up enough steam, before it had sufficient power to pull the trucks again.

Our train pulled into Wun Lun just before daylight. We were ordered off and told that the remaining seven kilometres to Chungkai had to be completed on foot. Half asleep, and cold, we picked our way along the track, as cautiously as the speed set by the Nips would allow. Most of us were barefooted and the remainder might just as well have been. Our ration carrying marches from Bondei had seen to that, canvas boots had not been intended for that sort of treatment.

We arrived at the entrance to Chungkai bund just as a party of several hundred men were leaving the camp for work. They told us Tamarkan bridge had also been destroyed and that the Nips had parties working on it, day and night, doing repairs. "You'll be on it tomorrow," they assured us, "whether you're sick or not". This was a fine reception after Bondei. "Surely this war must be nearly over at last!"

Chapter 24

"Nobby, Horse Doctor"

> *"The worst atrocities are probably committed by those who are most afraid."*
>
> Lord D'Abernon
> 1857–1941

Back in Chungkai yet again, we were subjected to the usual checks and searches, after which the Nips allowed the battalion RSM to sort out where we should go. Whenever the Nips called for a party to go up country, so called fit men may have been taken from the same working battalion but this wouldn't necessarily mean that they came from the same regiment. Frequently more than one working battalion was involved, and I often found myself working alongside men from other regiments, perhaps not meeting a fellow Cambridgeshire for months.

This was the Regimental Sergeant Major's task here, there were only two Cambridgeshires in this sick party, both of us being sent to the same working battalion, where we found two or three others from our unit. Other Cambridgeshires were in Chungkai at this time, some in another working battalion and several in the Camp hospital.

We received a small cob of rice bread and a spoonful of the mixture still being called jam, this was our breakfast, not much of it, but it went down well after the terrible food we had been getting over the past few weeks.

Off to see the British Medical Officer I discovered that unless you were nearly dead, it was work for everyone here.

Next day we learned the truth of the words spoken by the men on the bridge. A friend whose legs were swollen with beri beri, no boots on his feet, a very sick man, was sent to work on the bridge. How he marched there and worked from eight in the morning until nine forty five at night heaven only knows. I was put on a gardening job but didn't last the day out. I felt terribly ill and on reporting sick was found to have a temperature of one hundred and four. I had got BT Malaria. But I was lucky. Although never having the protection of a mosquito net, and never being able to do anything to avoid it, this was my first attack – some men had had as many as fifty by now.

The Nip MO, "Nobby," with "Ada", were a deadly pair, "Nobby", the officer, looked for all the world like a head lad in a racing stable, and was known to us as the "Horse doctor". "Ada", his interpreter, looked like a woman, and talked like one, but there the similarity ended. He would send half dead men to work without compunction. Sick parades were a farce. The number of sick men allowed "bed down" was regulated by the numbers "Nobby" chalked on a blackboard. He allowed each working battalion a certain number sick and when it was exceeded the unfortunate remainder were forced to work. I had to parade with many others to see if "Nobby" would give me "bed down". With a temperature of 104, and expecting to pass out at anytime, I struggled several hundred yards in the blazing sun to be examined, or inspected, by this Nip. The sick parades took place a few yards from his office, he didn't intend to walk very far. There were many other men, far worse than me, suffering from all manner of complaints and diseases, but it made no difference, "Nobby" would decide who would work. I was fortunate this time and allowed to have a couple of days off. "Nobby" never examined a man to my knowledge, I don't suppose he was a doctor or would have known what to do in any case. Rumour had it that he was really a vet, or had been an assistant to one. Sometimes he might check a pulse, or put his hand on a man's chest, to see if it was hot, but most times he would blink his slit eyes behind thick spectacles and check the numbers on his blackboard.

I remember on one occasion, a man suffering from quinzies being brought in front of him, the poor devil could hardly swallow, and was slobbering at the mouth. "Nobby" didn't want to know, as far as he was concerned the unfortunate man could work. The British MO protested vehemently and eventually "Nobby" relented and decided to look. He picked up a dirty piece of bamboo from the dusty ground, and tried to press it on the sufferer's tongue to look at his throat. Sometimes "Nobby" would demand that all men be turned out for one of his sick parades, keep them waiting about in the burning sun for ages and then not bother to turn up. Other times he would send along a Nip private who was usually worse than him. "Nobby" often had a purge of the hospital huts, in an effort to find more workers, turning out anyone he considered to be fit, even when they may not have had long to live.

He cut down the number of orderlies and only allowed a few men for any dispensing or laboratory work. Medical supplies were practically nil, or at least they weren't reaching the sick. I suspect "Nobby" was hoarding, or disposing of them elsewhere. The treatment for malaria, when I had my first attack, was ten grains of quinine a day for three days. This was only a partial cure, it did little to ward off the fever, and within a few days the victim would be just as bad again.

Quinine, very unpleasant to take at the best of times, was issued in powder form, many men would vomit at the mere thought of attempting to swallow the stuff. Whenever possible, I would scrounge a small piece of paper, make up my own quinine capsule and hopefully overcome the problem of the terrible taste.

Rice meals were never very appetising, but a man with malaria normally felt too ill to eat anything for several days, as a consequence he rapidly became weak and lost weight. Fever cases were usually allowed four or five days free from work, but after that were sent to the bridge, or to work on duties about the camp.

Malaria cases and many of the other "sick in lines" had to attend the Nip roll calls morning and night, even if it meant being carried there by their mates. It was not uncommon to see malaria cases fainting or vomiting while waiting for "Nobby" to appear. I will always remember a fellow Cambridgeshire, shivering under his rice sack in an uncontrollable rigor, bathed in perspiration. "Are you getting quinine Bob?" I asked. "Don't ask stupid questions," he implored, through teeth chattering like castanets, "You know very well you have to start smouldering before you get quinine in this bloody place".

The food in Chungkai was very short, but better than I had eaten in over a year. Breakfast was still the same small hard cob of rice bread baked in the camp and the midday meal plain rice and dhal beans. In the evening we usually had rice, and a quarter pint of fairly thick vegetable stew, sometimes with a little meat flavour, and often a "dufor" of some sort. We still received our drink of hot boiled water each meal. The portions dished up were always small, and in spite of scrounging here and there, I was always hungry, except when off my food because of malaria. Going to sleep hungry wasn't really a problem, we were usually exhausted anyway. I continued to dream about food and always woke up hungry in the morning. Still, perhaps we would be having decent food and plenty of it soon.

Work continued, repairing both the wooden and steel bridges at Tamarkan. Having described the Wampo bridge, in the previous chapter, as being typical of all the bridges we built in Thailand, it is necessary to qualify those remarks somewhat. Most bridges did follow a similar pattern, and the same degree of crudeness, being built over land, culverts, small ravines, or round the side of cliffs. The one exception was Tamarkan – the point where the railway crossed the Kwai Noi, a river some one hundred and seventy yards wide, but quite shallow overall. In the first place it had been crossed by a wooden bridge, very much on the lines of Wampo, Kanu and the others, but later by the construction of a more sophisticated effort, consisting of ten steel spans resting on concrete piers. I spent sometime working on these bridges, in between my now regular bouts of malaria, when according to "Nobby's" standards I was fit. We would leave Chungkai each morning at seven thirty, march along the track to the bridge, start work immediately on arrival, and get back to camp about nine thirty in the evening. We repaired the breaches in the steel bridge by using timber, a primitive looking scaffolding job. It would be almost ready to take a train when our planes came over in low level attack and blew several spans down again. The wooden bridge was bombed and put out of action, as fast as we could repair it. "Charlie" the recci plane carried out his daily observation, and knew exactly when to have them destroyed again.

My days on the steel bridge, were spent working under the direction of a slave driving Nip who we called the "Mad Carpenter". He had a vile temper, kept us working the whole time without breaks, muttering continuously, when he wasn't screaming orders in Japanese. He was forever hitting us with lumps of wood, for not working fast enough, or failing to understand what was expected of us. We did have a laugh one day, another Nip on the scaffolding worked himself up into such a rage, that he spat his false teeth into the river below. He was the only Nip I remember

Tamarkand Bridge.

DEE

The two bridges at Tamarkan, steel and wooden. The wooden construction preceded the steel, but in the latter stages of the war neither was operational due to the attention of allied planes. Goods and men were ferried over the river to trains on either side.

seeing with dentures, most of them had very good teeth, though with sometimes a generous show of gold fillings.

We were beaten every day, and some men even pushed into the river, by the furious and frenzied Nips. Whenever our planes came over, as they did most days, we raced off the bridge into the jungle as fast as we could go. More often than not the Nips were in the lead.

While the bridges were out of action, parties of us had to go to Tamarkan at night, and help ferry goods across the river. Trains were now only moving at night, because of the constant threat of aerial attack during daylight hours. The trains would come as far as the bridge on either side of the river, we would unload them, take the goods to the other side on small barges and re-load the other train.

Another arduous job involved carrying rations, and tubs of water, to Nips manning an anti-aircraft post, sited at the top of a very steep climb, overlooking the river and bridge.

A pleasant change was to find oneself included in a special working party to Kamburi, we looked upon it as a day out. After making the short journey by river in a "Pom Pom" towed barge, we would find a little civilisation, albeit only made up of natives.

The first time I went, the Nip in charge asked if there were any carpenters among us. A party of twenty five men, we told him not to insult us, we were all good carpenters. He was exceedingly pleased, it was his lucky day, he needed to build a bamboo hut and we were the ideal men for the job, get it done and he would have plenty of time to relax.

In a very short time the frame work was completed, it looked good, the Nip was all smiles. All that needed doing now was to apply atap thatch to the roof. Four men commenced the work. It wasn't proceeding quickly enough for our Nip. In spite of our protests, he ordered twenty men on to the roof. The inevitable happened, the whole structure came down and the Nip's temperature and temper went up. On return to camp he made it clear, through an interpreter, that he didn't want any of us to work for him again.

On other occasions I went to Kamburi working on air raid shelters for ration lorries. This was another comparatively easy job, we were normally left well alone by our Nip who obviously had more interesting things to do and left us to our own devices. Digging away with our native tools, in bare feet, heads unprotected from the broiling sun, there was always a certain amount of relaxation when the Nip's back was turned. "I'm getting quite expert with this chunkal," said one of our party, demonstrating his dexterity by chopping pieces of twig in two, "I'm as good as any bloody native. I could take off your toes as clean as a surgeon with a knife."

Down came the chunkal with terrific force, just short of someones bare foot.

"Right. Take off a couple of mine," said the owner of a foot, "and save me from going up country again. Only make a neat job of it. I hate a mess. Just below the joints will do." This sort of foolery was common. Down came the chunkal again with tremendous power; and, my God, three toes jumped away from the foot and lay in the dust like unshelled peanuts. How we stood like fools. Stunned for a moment. Then had the sense to apply a tourniquet made from someones Jap Happy, before rushing the injured man off to an MO, on a stretcher made from rice sacks.

Back in camp the main work meant gardening, and building pill boxes in the corners of the bund, obviously to keep us in. On most working parties the Nips were becoming more irritable, and served out beatings on the slightest provocation.

Sickness increased in camp, and the death rate mounted, men

were dying from all manner of complaints, blackwater fever, dysentery, beri beri, general anaemia, ulcers and malaria to name just a few. Except in very small quantities, medicine and drugs were unobtainable, medical officers had practically no medical supplies to work with, about all they could rely on was hope. Following my initial dose of malaria I joined the large majority of men suffering regular attacks. There would be several days of high fever, during which I would be excused work, the fever abated, it would be back to work for a few days, then down with another attack. Sometimes I received a few grains of quinine, but usually nothing at all. I was just one of many experiencing the same unpleasant routine, in fact nearly everyone was suffering from malaria in varying degrees.

I had now joined forces with two fellow Cambridgeshires, Bert Langham and Freddie Cudlip. We shared all our meagre possessions, even shared bouts of malaria! One of us was usually down with an attack, completely off our food, and the other two shared the ration. We stayed together the remaining months of the war, until we were able to enjoy our first taste of freedom.

But despite all hardships and disease, cheerfulness abounded. "If only those at home could see us now," we would say, as we surveyed our miserable conditions. Even the roll calls provided a little amusement. They were still held night and morning but had now become more of a formal affair. We all had to parade, by battalion, on the large open square, all the so called fit men and the sick not in hospital too. A rostrum had been built at one end of the square, and the presiding Nip would climb up to take the salute. A little light relief was afforded us when "Suspenders" took the parade. He was a Nip RSM, and he would appear resplendent in uniform from the knees upward, complete with his large sword. It was his bottom half that caused us such amusement. He wore brilliant white tennis shoes and short white socks, held up by gaily coloured suspenders, his shorts revealing a pair of skinny knees. He appeared to be tremendously proud of these suspenders, he certainly must have been the only person in Chungkai to possess a pair. He would take up his position on the platform, and on a word of command, all heads had to be turned toward him, and slightly bowed in salute.

The Nips had become almost apprehensive, they seemed to be scared that we were becoming too much aware of how events were progressing in the world outside. Frequent searches were made, although little of importance discovered. The hut piquets, introduced before I left for Bondei, were still very much part of the Chungkai scene, in fact they continued here and elsewhere until our release.

Rumours persisted that the war was nearly over in Europe. This was May 1945. Surely there must be some truth in the stories this time. We couldn't go on like this for ever, so many of our comrades had thought the same, and it seemed a lifetime since they had died. We weren't living, just existing, hanging on desperately till the day we were free again. Rumours became stronger. No longer were the sources saying "nearly" it was now supposed to be "completely". Surely that didn't mean our part of the world too? Many men scoffed at the idea, others thought it too good to be true. Our hopes had been raised before, and this time we wouldn't be taken in so easily. The rumours became stronger, and men returned to their huts claiming to having heard the news direct from the Nips, others would have heard it from "the well-dressed Thai". It was always a case of getting the story no less than fourth hand. We all wanted to believe it, but dare not build up hopes, to have them completely dashed within a few days. We then heard that all three cookhouses, British, Australian and Dutch, had been saving rations, in order to give us a Victory meal, as soon as the rumour had been confirmed. This was more promising, but, like many others, I still wasn't entirely convinced.

I never did know how the confirmation came about, but sure enough the Victory meal was laid on about 12 May. It should be pointed out that the cooking, and distribution of our food, was always carried out by POW's, the Nips seldom saw our meals. They probably wouldn't have noticed anything different about this one in any case. But it certainly was different! Each battalion received the meal in turn. The remaining battalions giving up some of their rations, until all men had been given this opportunity to celebrate the Allies' Victory in Europe. I went down with malaria at the start of my meal, so was not able to enjoy any of it. I had to be content with a glimpse of plenty of vegetables, and a rice concoction, baked in the shape of a 'V'.

Even after this evidence many of us could scarcely believe it to be true. I was not at all convinced. Later, I heard the padre offering a prayer of thanks-giving for the end of the war in Europe, and the removal of the threat to our homes.

I believed.

But when was it going to be our turn? Some of the Nips became more savage than ever in their treatment, but quite a number began to see the light and were turning out to be quite humane. One day while out on a working party, collecting wood by barge, one of our guards who spoke very good English, confirmed what we had been waiting to hear. "The war with Germany is over," he said "I wish I were an Englishman. What will happen to us do you think?" We told him we didn't believe it and as to his future who knows. Very little work was done that day.

Our planes came over even more frequently and the Nips became afraid of an organised break from the camp. They needn't have worried, it would have been very foolish on our part to attempt it. We were surrounded by jungle, the sea was miles away, and the countryside teeming with Nip troops. The Nip RSM, through his interpreter, told us several times, that it was the wish of the Great Nippon that we should eventually return to our homes in safety.

For once we saw eye to eye with the Great Nippon.

After dodging death from disease for so long, it was our intention to dodge death from bombs also. I for one, meant to avoid being the central figure in those forlorn groups, that could be seen making their way to the camp cemetery, two or three times a week.

Parties were still returning from up country, always in a shocking state of health, often within a few days of arrival many of them had died. Each day parties were still being sent to Tamarkan on bridge repairs, and "Charlie" still came over to watch their progress. If only the Nips would follow the example of the Germans and pack it in! Or were the Germans still fighting? Some said they were. Even now we were not all convinced. The reason for this was that our existence as prisoners went on just the same, and our mood of dejection increased when we heard we were to be moved yet again, to another camp, as Chungkai wouldn't be safe when the floods rose in September.

September, and now it was only May! Surely to God we should be free by September!

Chapter 25

Tamuang

"He that leaveth nothing to chance will do few things ill, but he will do very few things."

George Savile, Lord Halifax
1633–1695

Several times high ranking Nip Officers visited the base camps, and after one such visit, it became apparent that the rumours concerning the evacuation of Chungkai, were true. This time we were to be moved about ten kilometres down country, to a place called Tamuang. At least it was the right direction. The place had been used as a base camp for Number Four group, but according to all the rumour experts, Number Four group was moving still further down country. They were to build a smart new Red Cross camp, no doubt to impress the Allies, when the day of freedom arrived.

Preparations for the mass exodus from Chungkai commenced in late June 1945. All spare huts were taken down, and the bamboo and atap stacked outside the bund, ready to be transported by barge to Tamuang. Most of this work was carried out in addition to the normal days labours. We ate our evening meal, and then turned out to perform this "fatigue" until dark. All men classed as "light sick" were included, no matter what their complaint.

We three Cambridgeshires, were enjoying a rare couple of days free of malaria, when the names of men to make up the advance party was announced. We were on it, and weren't sorry, another change of scenery would help pass the time more quickly. I for one was pleased to be leaving Chungkai. But not all men would be moving, the Nips intended that some remain to look after the camp gardens, and also be available for work on the bridge.

We left Chungkai, travelling by river, the most pleasant move I had experienced to date. Until the building of the railway, river travel was probably the most important and efficient method of transportation in Thailand, or maybe I was never near enough to civilisation, to see any alternative operation involving the roads.

The barges in which we travelled, were similar to extra large rowing boats, with a covering of sorts in the centre. Several of these would be towed in line, behind a dilapidated motor boat. Each barge had a native squatting precariously in the rear, nonchalantly controlling a tiller with his bare foot. We called these motor boats "Pom Poms", I suppose because of their engine noise. They were a common sight, and often the towed barges were controlled by little children, many of them under school age. Some barges were punted up and down the river, by barefooted natives, walking along small ledges on the barge sides, using long bamboo poles.

Another common sight were very large rafts, made up of hundreds of bamboo poles lashed together, several rafts in line, making one long floating object, sixty yards or more in length. The native controlling one of these rafts, which was of course the method of bringing bamboo and timber down from the jungle, lived with his family in a little atap shelter, built on the rear raft. It was nothing unusual to see a meal being cooked outside their temporary home as the long cumbersome rafts moved slowly down stream, like a convoy of gigantic crocodiles. As the pom poms towed our barges away from Chungkai, I think most of us hoped we had seen the last of the place. At the same time we were naturally apprehensive of the future that awaited us, surely the next camp would be better, and our stay in it must be brief. Some of our guards had said that, "The Great Nippon Empire would fight the world alone". Perhaps, but not for long we thought.

It didn't take long to reach Tamuang, travelling with the current. In about an hour we were unloading the barges, our trip completed. Tamuang turned out to be a large camp, encircled by a bund, with another dividing it down the centre, separating POW's and Nips as at Chungkai. At least we wouldn't have to dig another darn great ditch! It was midway between the river and the main road, and to see Nip lorries and native "piggi" buses travelling up and down, provided me with my first glimpse of civilisation for three years. A few men of Number Four group remained but they moved down country within a few days of our arrival.

As advance party our job was, of course, preparing the camp for the mass of prisoners and Nips shortly to follow. Daily a number of barges arrived from Chungkai, stacked high with all manner of stores and equipment, which had to be unloaded and taken to various parts of the camp. Within a few days, more men began arriving and the amount of stores coming in increased too, in fact the job of unloading barges continued for weeks. As more so called fit men arrived, more huts were erected, and others given some badly needed repair.

Apart from this work, one of the main tasks we had to perform, during the first few weeks at Tamuang, was preparing and maintaining the camp gardens. Not gardening as one would expect in Britain. The tools were different, and the main crops grown, kajong, a creeping vine type spinach and sweet potatoes for their tops. The ground badly needed tilling, and the Nips found a home-made plough for us to use. I well remember the amusement caused, when we attempted to yoke an ox to this primitive implement. When we had succeeded in this part of the operation, it was almost impossible to get the beast to pull the plough, perhaps it didn't understand our language. No matter how much pulling, pushing and cajoleing tactics were used the animal refused to budge. We gave in, and resorted to the use of chunkals and POW power.

I continued to get my now regular attacks of malaria, with intervals of six to ten days between each. During these I worked, fit or not, like the majority of other POW's. I say "the majority of other POW's" for reasons which will shortly become apparent.

Fate dealt me an unkind blow one day, by arranging for me to work in a Nip clothing store. Along with several other men, I was given the job of moving hundreds of pairs of rubber boots. This was too much for me. I looked at the pair on my feet, I don't know why I was still wearing them. Completely worn out, toes protruding one end, heels the other, with nothing more than a few square inches of thin sole between, and held on my feet with odd bits of bamboo ties. In no time at all, I found a pair that I thought would fit, next I had to get them on my feet without that damned Nip seeing me. He was certainly conscientious, never seemed to take his eyes off us for many seconds at a time, but at last the opportunity came. First I hurriedly slipped my present footwear off and hid them behind some old rubbish. My idea was to put my new boots on, foul them with dirt to make them look old, slip out of the store wearing them, and return barefooted. This wouldn't be at all unusual, I was barefooted now, having discarded my old boots. But my plan went sadly wrong. I got the new boots on, fouled them, but that eagle eyed Nip didn't give me a chance to complete the operation. After about an hour he approached me, "Kurra" (come here) he bellowed, and pointing to my feet resplendent in new rubber boots, "Nanda".

He wanted an explanation.

I did my best to answer, as he bashed my face as hard as he could, punching me in the stomach, and anywhere else he fancied, making certain he remembered to kick my shins. I told him the truth. The Nips wouldn't give me anything to wear on my feet, and seeing all these boots, I decided to help myself, whose boots were they anyway, Red Cross?

He was several inches shorter than me, and as he bashed me I trembled with rage, even in my unfit condition, I believe I could have murdered him, but we had learned not to retaliate. Take the bashing with as much dignity as possible, and remain passive, that was the proven policy. He made me stand to attention at the end of the store, with the new boots hanging round my neck. He said he would hand me over to the Kempies. I knew what to expect if the notorious Nip police got me. I stood to attention the rest of the day. He came and bashed me occasionally, as did any passing Nip fancying a bit of fun. I don't know where I ached or hurt most, and "Blimey, could I do with a drink". When the day's work ended, he gave me another bashing and said, "No good pinchi pinchi soldier, keep boots, not work in my store again." I returned to my hut and my pals told me they thought I had been run over by a bus!

The Nip was true to his word, if ever he found me included in a group allocated to work with him, it was always the same. "No want him, he pinchi pinchi soldier!" Still, I had won myself a pair of boots!

"Charlie" the recci plane continued his visits and bombers were over most days. Several times they dropped leaflets, and some did reach prisoner's hands although it was a punishable offence to be caught with one. They were intended for the local population and no doubt Nips too, printed in foreign languages they depicted strange tanks and landing craft, the likes of which weren't in existence when we became prisoners, some three and a half years before.

The bridge at Tamarkan still received plenty of attention, bombed as fast as it was repaired. Parties were sent daily on repair work, leaving camp at about four in the morning, they wouldn't return until ten in the evening or later. Another party, with a few Nips, returned to Chungkai, they were to be available for repair work on the bridge and ferrying supplies across the river when the bridges were out of action.

Chapter 26

No Good House

"God defend me from my friends; from my enemies I can defend myself."
Proverb 16th Century

Within a few days of my bashing for stealing the boots, I had yet another reminder that our war wasn't over yet. This time from a totally different sequence of events and characters. All the morning we had been harried by a Nip Sergeant, known to us as "Joe Tunny", he was as mad as a hatter, and had reduced our working party to desperation. Our job was unloading barges. We had been at it without a break since breakfast, were hungry, thirsty and most of us near exhaustion. Returning to our hut for a midday meal of rice and stew, I had collected mine, sat on the end of my bed platform, raised a spoonful of the unappetising stuff to my mouth, when I heard from the other end of the hut.

"Outside Joe Tunny's party."

My God. So we weren't even to have a break and a meal.

"Outside Joe Tunny's party," bellowed the voice, a little nearer this time. The voice belonged to "Ginger", a British Sergeant Major. For months we had suffered from this individual. Many of us thought he was worse than some of the Nips. He never did a stroke of work apart from supplying them with the numbers available for the working parties. As far as we were concerned he was fat, over-fed by our standards, and far too anxious to please the Nips. At least he was careful to make certain that if any heads were to be bashed, his wouldn't be among them.

"Outside Joe Tunny's party", this time much closer. This was too much for me. I shouted aloud what one normally says under one's breath to a sergeant major.

"Who said that?"

"I did", I replied, and added a few more unflattering remarks concerning him and Joe Tunny.

"Report to my office when you finish your days work," he fumed.

I thought little more of it, and returned to work with the rest of the party, snatching a few minutes during the afternoon to eat our now cold, tasteless meal. That evening I reported to the office, a section at the end of a hut, partitioned off with bamboo and atap, also serving as sleeping quarters for "Ginger" and the RSM in overall charge of our working battalion. I expected to receive an admonition from Ginger for my rude remarks earlier in the day.

I got a surprise.

I appeared before the RSM who looked very much to me like "Ginger's" mouthpiece. In next to no time, I had been sentenced to serve seven days detention in the Nips' "No Good House", during which time I was not to receive any pay. In less than ten minutes, I was crawling on my hands and knees to enter the cell, the bamboo cage, which was to be my home for the next seven days and nights.

So this was what the "No Good House" was like from the inside. The door through which I had entered, was about twenty four inches high by fourteen inches wide, good job it was me getting in and not that fat slob "Ginger", he wouldn't have got his backside through the opening. The cell was one of several constructed side by side, in a small hut of bamboo and atap. The sides and top were made of tightly lashed bamboo poles, and the interior dimensions about six feet high, six feet long and four feet wide. A man of average height could just stand up and lay down. There was no sleeping platform, just the dusty earth floor. The toilet was a hole scratched in one corner, and one hoped that the previous occupant had not found it necessary to avail himself of the non-existent facility too often, and that much time had elapsed since the place was last used.

The "No Good House" was dark, dirty and smelly, but afforded one plenty of time to think. My immediate thoughts were that I must be dreaming. Surely this couldn't be true! Bad enough being put in here by the Nips, but had I really been put into this place by my own people? What was my serious offence? Was it a crime not to want to work for the Nips? Perhaps when the war was over I would be given a new army pay book, which would contain the entry, or citation "Awarded for showing reluctance to work for the enemy. Seven days detention in the "No Good House"." Surely the Nips, especially "Joe Tunny", would have a laugh if they knew. Supposing news came through that the war was over, no longer a prisoner of the Nips, would I remain a prisoner of the British?

Times of adversity bring out the best and worst in men's characters. Great courage, selflessness and comradeship abounded in all the camps in which I worked, but there was sometimes another side. Men whose behaviour in normal times might be beyond reproach, showed tendencies toward selfishness, greed and the determination to survive at all cost, even at the expense of fellow comrades' lives. Although I must stress that these individuals were in the minority, it is fair to say they could be found amongst all ranks, from the private soldier to officers. It was a case of the old army maxim "Up ladder Jack, I'm all right."

In the "No Good House" I must confess that the sergeant major "Ginger" occupied my thoughts for the first few hours at least. He wasn't in my regiment, probably not even a genuine Sergeant Major, I did know of men moving from one camp to another, promoting themselves on the way. Others had been "promoted" whilst prisoners, I'm not sure how this was indeed possible, although according to some we were still on active service. Among us other ranks, there was a term for these POW promotions – "Rice Stripes". I had only come across this individual on arriving at Tamuang, but he was typical of several senior NCO's I had met. Some of them always managed to escape the up country working parties. All the "cushy" jobs around the camps appeared to be taken by senior NCO's. The cookhouses were full of them, and naturally that was where the best food, our main source of survival,

DEE

The 'No Good House'. It was necessary for the prisoner occupant to crawl in on his hands and knees.

was to be found. I remember one Sergeant Major who, in different circumstances, had a particularly loud mouth. He was always chasing the underdog, and ever ready to have him slapped on charge. When I had last seen him, at one of the base camps, he had a job as sanitary man, clearing up the mess of men unable to reach the latrine in time.

I often wondered who it was selected the names of men to go up country, when it was not just a question of who must remain behind. Who received my pay when I didn't get any, it must have gone somewhere!

I remembered another small incident which took place nearly three years before, nothing to do with a senior NCO this time. It was way back in Changi shortly after we had moved there. I was recovering from dysentery, and still unable to walk but a few yards.

"Want anything from the canteen Jack?" asked another member of my unit. Grateful at the offer I replied, "Yes please, five cents of peanuts," and handed him a ten cent note, all the money I possessed.

He returned sometime later and passed me the small quantity of nuts. "Thanks" I said, and waited for the five cents change. "Change? You don't get any change mate, thats my charge for fetching them," he told me.

I also remembered travelling to River Valley camp, arriving there, and finding that all the kit I had managed to collect, after my spell in Alexandra Hospital, had been stolen by other POW's, and I was left with all I stood up in.

Yes, the veneer of decent behaviour can be very thin in times of adversity.

It would be unjust to give the impression that all senior NCO's were shirkers, some of them were very fine men. Snowy, who I have mentioned earlier was one of the best I had the privilege to know. He wasn't a big man, had very blonde hair, but was tough and courageous. I first saw Snowy back in England, he was covered in soot, having just cleaned the flue of a chimney stack at Weeting Hall in Norfolk. When I was in the Regimental Aid Post, after receiving the burns, Snowy was brought in, he had sweated blood in action, I always thought it just a phrase until I saw his back and chest. It was always good to be in his working party, he slogged away with the rest of us, and was never frightened to stand up to the Nips. He was a demon barber, and would risk eating anything with "sugar on it", sometimes with near disastrous results. Always in the Quiz team, he could lecture on Darwin's theory, or anything else for that matter.

Inevitably perhaps, I thought of home. How were the family now? Perhaps some of them may have died or indeed been killed in air raids. All mail received by POW's was normally more than a year old, and very brief at that. But they would never guess where I was at present. Anyway they wouldn't have heard of a "No Good House".

For some unknown reason I thought of a near total eclipse of the sun. Perhaps it was because of my present abode, being very gloomy and dark. I couldn't remember where exactly I was when it happened the previous year, but it had certainly been a disturbing experience at the time. The jungle is never quiet. There is always the incessant whistle of crickets and other insects, the hum of bees, mosquitoes and the deep throated croak of bull frogs. After a while one becomes oblivious to the sounds around them. On this particular day, I was returning to camp, through the jungle, when in a matter of seconds near darkness descended. I'll never forget that eerie feeling, as all jungle noises abruptly ceased. Everywhere was completely silent for what seemed an age, until the sun emerged again. I hadn't the faintest idea what was happening, thought the world must be coming to an end, hadn't been warned and didn't realise it was an eclipse of the sun.

Overall my spell in the "No Good House" was pretty uneventful. With my tattered groundsheet in direct contact with the earth floor, and my rice sack for covering, I slept soundly most nights. I found it more comfortable than the bamboo platforms, and certainly free of the bugs that infested them. Although I had ants to contend with, and the ever present lice, which accompanied one everywhere, at least I wasn't visited by any unfriendly centipede, or scorpion, which were a terrific size over here. I did have another visitor, however, a very welcome one. Each night, just after dark, a slight scratching and tapping at the back of my cell, would precede the passing of a lighted cigarette, through a small hole we had made for this purpose. No words were exchanged, speech was unnecessary, besides too much noise might have led to Jack Darking, another pal of mine, being caught.

Before my sentence was finished, I had another attack of malaria, but remained in the "No Good House". Perhaps that place was as good as anywhere in the circumstances, at least I wasn't working. I did receive a small quantity of quinine, but, my God! How I could have done with half a dozen good blankets, to prevent me from shivering, when the rigors came on.

Back in my hut, not noticeably any worse for my spell of detention, life continued in more or less the same humdrum way, work, eat, sleep and hope. Food began to improve, but as the quality went up, the quantity went down. It was still rice and stew, with the occasional dufor; very little of it, but at last our cooks were becoming proficient in the art of cooking the stuff. "Leggi queues" were a common sight in all parts of the camp, I joined them between my attacks of malaria. I don't think there could have been a grain of rice wasted in the camp.

Now and again we managed to get a duck's egg, thanks to the good offices of a Dutchman who was in charge of several hundred ducks, the Nips kept on the camp. Generosity to his many friends, eventually brought the Dutchman into trouble with the authorities, who realised they were not getting anywhere near the number of eggs, they were entitled to expect. "Why no eggs, soldier?" asked the Nip. "Ducks Yasumi," replied the Dutchman, "No, lay eggs all the time."

"Canaro, bugaro," bellowed the indignant Nip.

"I speak when ducks Yasumi you speak all ducks lay eggs".

"But Nippon," protested the Dutchman, "Half the ducks, Mr Ducks, no lay eggs."

The Nip could think of no answer to this, except to beat the Dutchman, which probably relieved his feelings, but failed to produce more eggs.

We still managed to get a smoke, but tobacco was now a heavy price, half a weeks pay would buy enough to make fifteen to twenty cigarettes. Papers were unobtainable, and we used anything we could scrounge. A notice put up in the camp, would disappear within a few minutes, and quickly become cigarette papers. Books stolen from Nip quarters, met the same end, the pages distributed, made into cigarettes, and even smoked before they were missed.

Chapter 27

Good News

"As cold waters to a thirsty soul, so is good news from a far country."
Proverbs 25.25

By the end of July 1945, Tamuang had progressively become one of the best camps I'd been in. Several months had passed without a party being sent up country, rumour had it that no more were to go. In fact several parties did leave camp, but in the opposite direction. No one seemed to know exactly where they went, but the general opinion considered that it was to a much better place, and that before very long we would all be following. Most of the work in the camp had become comparatively easy, and for the benefit of the camp in general. No longer were we all having to work from dawn to dark. We had even been going to the river, for our end of day wash and swim, under the watchful eyes of Nip escorts.

But this bathing parade had now been cancelled, and in its place the Nips substituted a night fatigue. We paraded for our evening roll call, then all went to the river to wash, and each man had to bring back bamboo for building, or logs for the cookhouse fires. In addition other parties were employed unloading this wood from barges, often working until well after dark, whatever the weather, which to mention too often, becomes monotonous, but was quite often, exceedingly wet.

I was working on one of the evening "unloading parties", when there was yet another reminder that the war was not over, and I witnessed a typical example of Nip brutality. It made me thankful that I had never retaliated, when they beat me up. It was a wet night, and as usual, like most of the others, I was working in Jap Happy and bare feet; the boots I had stolen having long since worn out. A number of us were dragging bamboos from the river. The poles were slimy, the river bank slippery with mud, and it was also beginning to get dark. The Nips were shouting and screaming with their "Speedo's" and "Canaro's" and clumping us with lumps of bamboo, because the work wasn't proceeding quick enough for their liking. There were too many of us working in the confined area, men were slipping and sliding all over the place, and tempers on all sides were frayed. Looking back, the scene must have been very comical, had our circumstances not been those of prisoners of war.

An Australian, having difficulty keeping his feet, didn't move quick enough for a Nip sergeant. He hit the prisoner across the backside with a piece of stick to hurry him up. Without thinking, the Australian grabbed the stick, and broke it across his knee. This sent the Nip mad. He hit the unfortunate prisoner, with everything he could lay his hands on, smashing him in the face with a wooden "clomper", and hitting him all over the body with the butt end of a rifle he had snatched from a Korean guard. When the victim fell to the ground, he kicked him from head to foot. He would probably have killed him, had not some fellow Nips intervened, and dragged the savage creature away.

Interception by us would have been completely futile. Even if the whole camp revolted, there were now thousands of Nip troops in the area, more than a match for un-armed, near emaciated prisoners. In fact several Nips saw to it that the Australian was taken quickly back to camp for treatment. I saw him next day, he had a broken arm, was a mass of bruises, and could only hobble about with great difficulty.

The majority of the Nips, however, began to change their attitude altogether. The Koreans especially seemed to think "the writing was on the wall," as far as they were concerned.

Many quite openly expressed hatred of the Japanese, thinking no doubt that the war would soon end, and it might be in their interest to become much more friendly toward us, after all the roles could be reversed before long.

Conditions in Tamuang continued to improve. Old cookhouses were pulled down, and new ones built. These cookhouses should perhaps, be described in a little more detail, as they were typical of all cookhouses to be found in most of the larger camps. They were usually sited as near to the river as possible, for obvious reasons, river water was used for all purposes. It was a convenient place to wash cooking utensils, dump innocuous swill, and receive supplies from the Thai traders' barges.

The cookhouses were nothing more than atap shelters or shacks. An atap roof, supported on bamboo poles, covering a cooking area housing several quallies. These were large iron, bowl shaped containers, or great frying pans, about three feet in diameter and ten to twelve inches deep in the centre. The quallies were supported on, or rather built into fire places made from mud and rocks. Everything was cooked in these things, easy perhaps, as the meals seldom varied from our basic rice and stew. In addition to boiling, they were also used for frying rissoles or dufors, when such luxuries were available. Rice was usually boiled until most of the water had been absorbed, or evaporated leaving a crustation of burnt rice, round the bottom half of the quallie. There was a great demand for this, as a little extra delicacy, and it was never difficult for the cooks to dispose of it. The burnt rice, when even a little more burnt, was some times made into a form of drink, with added hot water. Rather deceptively known to us as coffee. Most of the cookhouses now had primitive ovens, improvised from gulamalacca tins, again built into fireplaces of mud and stone.

The Nip name for a cookhouse was "sweejabah", and for food "mishi". A saying often used by them was, "Mishi, mishi, taxan julto", which we understood to mean "The food good and plenty of it". It must have been a wrong translation! In addition to the cookhouse replacements, a number of the older huts were pulled down and new ones erected. Work was started on building a covered altar for church services. This was a radical change. Religious services had been forbidden by the Nips for some time, but recently they had relented, and were allowing one service to be held on Yasumi days. The same applied to a camp theatre. All entertainment of this kind had been banned for months. It was earlier in the year, back at Chungkai, where Turtleneck the interpreter, had stopped the show and had the stage dismantled. The Nips at that time appeared to think that we should not be happy or sing, especially as they weren't finding much themselves to sing about. That was all changing. Now a covered stage had been built several feet above the ground, on which the audience would sit in a semi-circle. Our camp administrators, POW that is, were instructed to organise a concert party, and be prepared to put on shows again. The Nips also told us to make a football pitch, this amounted to little more than putting up improvised goal posts at each end of the parade ground, but things were certainly looking up.

The place was being smartened up and made to look quite respectable, even to the extent of laying out ornamental gardens, complete with fancy bridges.

They allowed more men to be sick, or perhaps I should say, forced fewer sick men to work, they even allowed the sick more time to recover from their illnesses.

A number of books supplied by the American Red Cross, appeared in the camp, and a few allocated to each working party. Food was becoming very short, and we wondered if this too, might be a good sign. Was it perhaps, due to the attention our aircraft had been paying to Nip supply lines, if there was a shortage, we would be the first to feel any effect of it.

All these changes in attitudes and conditions, led us to believe that the end of the war must be getting a lot nearer, surely the Nips wanted to show the world how well they had treated their prisoners. Rumours were rife all over the camp, each day brought new ones, but never any confirmation.

I was working in the ornamental gardens, on about the 12 August 1945, when the rumour went round like wild fire that the war was over. For days we had been arguing whether it was true or not that Russia had declared war on Japan.

"What are we waiting for?" We threw down our tools.

"The Nips should be working for us!" We stood about laughing, and contemplating our imminent freedom, until a Nip shouted to us to get back to work.

"Go and tell that poor devil," some said pityingly, "he doesn't know its over."

But we didn't believe either. We picked up our tools and started again. There wasn't much work done, we had plenty to think and talk about, surely it couldn't be true? Yet it had to finish sometime. How would we know?

During the next few days the rumour persisted, there must be something in it this time, yet it seemed impossible. We remained prisoners, there were still the roll calls night and morning, and the same work to perform, although it was far from being hard. Then came more hopeful signs, there was an issue of clothing. American Red Cross stores that the Nips had presumably been sitting on for some time. Many men received new shirts and shorts. Every man got a new ready made Jap Happy, and our near naked bodies, now more the colour of the natives, through daily exposure to the sun, were covered once more. Yes, this surely must be a sign of the end. The Nips obviously wanted to show how well we had been treated.

August 16th was fixed as a Yasumi day, and the Nips ordered a football match in the afternoon, and a concert in the evening. On Yasumi morning there was another surprise. Every man was given a piece of toilet soap. This was the height of luxury, the first issue of its kind in three and a half years, at least as far as I was concerned. Ten cigarettes, "tailor-made" too. Incredible, and if this were not enough – a white handkerchief each. We'd forgotten there was such a thing. Where the hell had the Nips been hiding the stuff? It was obviously Red Cross supplies which should have been issued to us in the first place.

The football match was quite a farce, an international, Britain v Holland, many men played in bare feet, but most wore their brand new shirts that had just been issued. It roused terrific enthusiasm, but the concert in the evening attracted only a few hundred out of the two thousand men in camp. I was sitting at the edge of the crowd, not taking too much notice, until almost by magic, the audience trebled in number and excitement mounted high. The unfortunate performers were unable to make themselves heard, above the babble of voices, as hundreds of men began to crowd round and on the stage. It was obvious that something very important was about to happen, and I think most of us began to anticipate what it was to be.

The show was stopped. The compere announced that the CO, a British RSM, had something important to say. He came on to the stage, and in a deathly hush started to speak. He said, "The latest rumour in the camp" – that was enough. Nobody waited to hear more. Tremendous cheers rent the air and continued for many minutes. It was taken for granted that the war had ended at last. Men went "mad", jumped and shouted, patted, or rather, thumped each other on the back, waved brand new shirts as recklessly as if they had a wardrobe full of them, and shook hands with anyone near. My pal told me afterwards, I nearly broke his bones with my handshake, and felled him to the ground, with what was meant to be a jovial pat on the back. Not bad, considering a couple of days before I had been weak with malaria.

The stage became crowded with bodies, and it was a long time before the RSM could get everyone quiet again. Eventually he was able to tell us that the war had ended. We sang our National Anthem, at least most of us tried, it wasn't easy with a darn great lump in ones throat. The Dutch anthem followed, then the American, and for the benefit of the Australians "Land of Hope and Glory" though God knows why. Cheering broke out again, and several Union Jacks and Dutch flags appeared on the stage as if from a conjurer's hat.

After a while, and much difficulty, comparative quiet was restored, and this time the Padre appeared. He said a few words of prayer, during which the quietness that descended was deafening. We all sang "Abide with me". It could have been heard miles away. It was a moment those of us present will never forget. And, I do mean never. Our emotions were almost numb. All the years we had waited for this. It was almost impossible to grasp what had happened. After all the misery and deprivation, the living in squalor with death only a rice meal away, it wouldn't be long before we would be in touch with the outside world again. We lucky ones should soon be home, we thought of many of our friends, they would remain here for ever. There were men unashamedly crying, with tears streaming down their faces, others hysterical with delight. Many just stood about looking blank and bewildered, not yet able to grasp that the nightmare was as good as over. The concert party led, or rather endeavoured to lead, the crowd in community singing. They found it a hopeless struggle, most men were singing, but there were many impromptu groups, rendering all manner of songs, and most far from being melodious.

With my pals I returned to our hut. It was no more than two hundred yards away, but it took us an age to get there. Every few yards prisoners were celebrating the news, in their own particular way. The Nips saluting rostrum was over turned, small bonfires were burning all over the place. Someone scaled the Nip observation tower, and hung a Union Jack from it. I felt an urgent need to visit a latrine. Impossible. They were all occupied. The evening's events were having similar effect on many a nervous system!

Back in the huts the mood of excitement showed no sign of abating. Old scores amongst fellow prisoners were forgotten, there were hand shakes all round, good luck wishes, the future looked good, and there was plenty to talk about and look forward to.

Just before midnight our hut commander arrived, it was obvious he had something to say, but we weren't in any mood for a lecture. At last comparative silence was secured, and he said that orders had been received from the Nips – the Nips? – Yes of course, the Nips – Why, in our excitement we'd never even thought of beating them up! Their quarters were no distance, it wasn't too late now. Yes, there were still Nips! – They had sent for our Camp CO, the RSM, who had given us the news. They told him that the war was not yet over, and might not be for some time. No Armistice had been signed, and fighting could start again at anytime. We were still prisoners, and were to carry on as usual. Roll Call would be at the same time tomorrow, and working party parades were to continue as before. "Carry on as usual," we were told, "it is the only sensible thing to do for the next few days. You will all get extra clothes and food."

Of course, we thought, the Nips knew it was over, they had been frightened by the evening's events. They wanted to delay the hand over, and keep us quiet as long as possible, while they made their get away to escape our vengeance.

The Union Jack was taken down from the tower. We tried to sleep but not many men did, I couldn't, nor did I much for the next few nights.

Suddenly England seemed much nearer.

Chapter 28

Freedom

*"I only ask to be free.
The butterflies are free."*
Charles Dickens
1812–1870

The following morning everything seemed back to normal, it was almost as though nothing had happened. We went on the roll call as usual, and a young Nip officer took the salute, from the now righted rostrum. I began to think I must have been dreaming. If I had, then everyone else had shared the same dream. We were all discussing the previous nights celebrations, and wondering what would happen next. We didn't see the usual crowd of Nips, waiting to be allocated working parties, in fact none came into our area at all. We went about the usual work of camp improvements, but this time with little or no supervision from our own NCO's. Not a lot of work was done, but at least we were occupied, and a degree of discipline maintained. This was important, because in our state of excitement, and uncertainty, all manner of unpleasant and dangerous situations could have developed. There were still thousands of armed Nips in the area.

This unreal situation continued for several days, we seldom saw a Nip, those occupying the other side of the bund had acted with great restraint, or else they were frightened to come near us.

A wireless set was smuggled into camp, and the news given to us quietly each day. Even with this, we were unable to confirm if the war was over or not. Our meals improved several hundred per cent, the RSM CO obtained a few thousand dollars from the Nip commandant, for buying extra food, and everyday, numbers of native Piggi buses entered the camp. They brought in loads of

TO ALL ALLIED PRISONERS OF WAR

THE JAPANESE FORCES HAVE SURRENDERED UNCONDITIONALLY AND THE WAR IS OVER

WE will get supplies to you as soon as is humanly possible and will make arrangements to get you out but, owing to the distances involved, it may be some time before we can achieve this.

YOU will help us and yourselves if you act as follows :—

(1) Stay in your camp until you get further orders from us.

(2) Start preparing nominal rolls of personnel, giving fullest particulars.

(3) List your most urgent necessities.

(4) If you have been starved or underfed for long periods DO NOT eat large quantities of solid food, fruit or vegetables at first. It is dangerous for you to do so. Small quantities at frequent intervals are much safer and will strengthen you far more quickly. For those who are really ill or very weak, fluids such as broth and soup, making use of the water in which rice and other foods have been boiled, are much the best. Gifts of food from the local population should be cooked. We want to get you back home quickly, safe and sound, and we do not want to risk your chances from diarrhoea, dysentry and cholera at this last stage.

(5) Local authorities and/or Allied officers will take charge of your affairs in a very short time. Be guided by their advice.

Leaflet dropped over some camps advising prisoners of impending release and what action to take.

bananas, other fruit, and all manner of vegetables. We were soon getting more than we could eat. All the leggi queues vanished over night. Officers arrived from their POW camp at Kanburi, and took over the administration of our side of Tamuang. They told us that the war was as good as over, but that the armistice had not yet been signed. There were only a few Allied parachutists in various parts of Thailand, whereas there were thousands of Nip troops, all fully armed. Of course there were the Nips on the other side of the bund, and they still had their arms too.

We learned that the Thais had been planning a general rising against the Nips. A few Allied parachutists had been dropped in the area several months previously, they had been receiving arms and supplies from low flying planes at night. Quite a large number of Thais had received some sort of training, and were now armed in readiness for a general rising or revolt against the Nips. Hopefully this was to have taken place before the end of August. The plan appeared to have been, to kill all prison camp guards, then release and arm us. A large number of casualties had been expected, but there was a genuine fear that if the Allies were to make any advance in the area, the Japanese plan was to kill all prisoners of war. Their answer had been to have the bunds built round the camps and by so doing make it an easy task for them to bring about our total liquidation at the appropriate moment. A sobering thought. It would appear we were lucky to be alive.

The officers warned us that the Nips were still responsible for us, and at present we remained their prisoners. Their advice was, "To carry on as normal until more information can be obtained". Easier said than done, in our mood of excitement and impatience. But most of us saw it as sound advice, and realised that after more than three and a half years, it would be reckless, stupid and futile to do otherwise.

Meanwhile sickness continued, but "Nobby's" sick parades were out. Our own MO's took over completely, and were able to do as they pleased. Medical supplies that had been held by the Nips, much of them Red Cross supplies intended for our use in the first place, were released. I started another attack of malaria on 20 August, but this time received adequate doses of quinine.

One morning, excitement mounted high in the camp again. We were able to see and talk to the first two free British we had seen for years. They were an officer and a corporal. Both had been parachuted into Thailand, and would be staying in our camp to operate a radio transmitter. At last we would be in immediate touch with the world outside. The corporal had a bottle of whisky which we made short work of, and a few of us received a genuine "player" cigarette. They wore green uniforms which were strange to us, and the corporal carried a gun, the like of which we had never seen or used in our days as combatants. How long had it been since the fall of Singapore?

Both the officer and the corporal were bombarded with questions, to such an extent, that they couldn't cope, and the officer promised to give us a talk on Britain the following evening. He said he would do his best to answer any questions submitted. They thought we looked very strange in our Jap Happies and bare feet, but they looked just as unusual to us. We had our lecture, but the officer confessed it was impossible to answer all the questions, so many had been sent in, but he did his best to make up for our years of news starvation. Oddly enough the questions repeated the greatest number of times had been:

"Was it true that Deana Durbin was dead?"
"Was she killed in a car crash or had she died in childbirth?"
"Was it true that Shirley Temple was married and had a baby?"
"Had there been any rises in British Army Pay?"
"Had 'Lord Haw Haw' been shot by the Jerries as a British Agent?"

Every evening the news was read out to us, and we heard of various plans that were being made for our repatriation. The radio bulletins maintained that the Nips were to remain responsible for us, until we were eventually freed, but we were very anxious to see them disarmed.

Then we heard about the Atomic bomb that had finished the mighty Nippon. It seemed incredible and unbelievable to us, that just one bomb could have caused such a turn about in our fortunes, the officer had to devote a special talk on how it all came about.

The days seemed like weeks. After all the excitement on the night of the concert, our day of departure from Thailand, and the prison camps, still seemed a decade away. Surely we must be completely free soon. Changes in camp administration were continually coming into effect, although not fast enough for us. Eventually the Nips ceased to carry out guard duties, made themselves scarce, and confined themselves strictly to their own part of the camp. They looked very dejected and miserable, but some of the Koreans seemed overjoyed. Many Nips, who had been responsible for serious beatings of prisoners disappeared, perhaps it was just as well they did. One or two did receive hidings from our men, among them the "Admiral" who, whilst in charge of the barges, had broken the jaws of several men with his vicious blows. I looked in vain for the particular Nip I wanted to interview.

Those Nips remaining had to wait to have their rations issued by our camp quartermaster. The tables had definitely turned. But what an amazing and crazy situation it seemed to be, they were still the only ones with the arms. British and Dutch POW's took over the Nip guardroom, and became responsible for general discipline in the camp. Nip stores were taken over by POW's, and clothing, Red Cross stores, and medical supplies dated 1942 were handed out. The Union Jack and several other flags now flew from the top of the observation tower, and various other parts of the camp. No longer did we have to tolerate the Nip bugle calls, it was good to hear the efforts of a British bugler again, even if he was somewhat out of practice.

The river was open to us nearly all day, but officers advised us to keep within the camp boundary. There were many good reasons for this, they said, although it wasn't made too plain exactly what they were at the time. However, in fairness to them, I would say it was the correct advice. I shudder to think what may have happened, had two thousand or so deprived POW's, been allowed to descend, unrestricted, on the town and local population.

I think it should be said at this juncture, that in the circumstances prevailing, the uncertainty and unreality of the situation, the Nips in their quarters with guns, and us in ours unarmed, the discipline of POW's in Tamuang was excellent. Perhaps we had come so far, and had no intention of throwing it all away now. We received several grants of five dollars each, and were able to spend our new found wealth at the hundreds of little Thai stalls that now appeared along the road to the river. The prices of goods, mainly fruit, and some food, had also increased out of all proportion, now that the natives realised we had a little money to spend.

Parties of prisoners began to arrive from up country, many in a shocking state. When the first party arrived, volunteers were called for to help carry sick men, and stretcher cases into the camp. It was as though we were going back in time to 1943, when conditions were perhaps at their worst. The men were barely recognisable as human beings, most of them were Dutch Eurasions, although some were British. Their thin wasted bodies were filthy, and covered in sores. Many could barely stand, let alone walk. Most had beards and long matted hair, some with the evidence of dysentery running down, or dried on their legs. The stench was indescribable and sickening. Neither the Nips, nor the prisoners knew that the war was over, until they arrived at the camp. One of the Nips in charge was bawling and bullying men who could hardly muster enough strength to crawl, when he received the surprise of his life. A British POW, standing nearby, promptly smacked him round the ear a couple of times, and he was bundled off to our camp Nips, to receive an up date of news. The Nip was very fortunate, as were many of the others. The sight of these human skeletons, descending from the trucks, was unforgettable, our animosity toward the Nips was revived, could we ever forgive them for allowing such human misery and pain? Considering the hatred we felt at that time, those Nips could have been killed on the spot. Perhaps we were forgetting too easily what had gone before.

In spite of the disgusting state of these men, it was noticeable how dull sunken eyes, lit up with new hope, when they realised that the war was over. This was the end of the worst for them. They were cleaned up, fed, crammed with the now available medical treatment, and within a few days most were making progress toward recovery. Unfortunately several died within a few days of arriving, and there were still deaths each day among the sick already in the camp. We had parties working daily in the cemetery, in an effort to make it a fit resting place for the hundreds of our friends who would not return home. A service was held in their memory.

Several Thais and a Red Cross official visited the camp. He said he was disgusted at what he saw, but he was promptly assured that this place was heaven, to what it had been, with the Nips in charge, and bore no similarity to the terrible camps up country. He told us that no Red Cross official had been allowed to visit any of the camps, during the three and a half years of our captivity. We could have told him that. We did. And more. Such as what had happened to all the Red Cross issues intended for us, but which ended up being enjoyed by the Nips, or hoarded. He said we smelled like natives. This wasn't in the least surprising, we'd been living worse than animals for years. He was given a midday meal, one that by this time had improved out of all recognition. He thought it was terrible and couldn't eat it.

"Ah, I see you have milk in your tea," he commented.

"You're not in the NAAFI now mate," we told him, "that's not even tea, its boiled muddy water from the river!"

Under the instructions of the Para Officer, we made our camp recognisable from the air, by spreading a large Union Jack on the ground and marking POW in twenty feet black letters on a yellow background, using pitch, mercurechrome, chalk and curry powder for the purpose. We could have done with that curry powder earlier!

A fighter plane dived low over the camp as if to inspect our handiwork, we rushed out in the open to wave and it dipped its wings in salute. We were told the day and time on which we could expect supplies from the air, and a large part of the camp was kept clear for the purpose. We all turned out to watch, and it was a day to remember, when five Dakota aircraft appeared.

They circled the camp several times, and then came in low, dropping bundles on parachutes into the prepared spot. Over two hundred bundles were dropped, including food, clothing, medical supplies and a complete blood transfusion apparatus, with bottles of blood donated only two days before. We excitedly enjoyed the display, waving shirts or anything that came to hand, airmen appeared at the open doors of the planes waving in return.

Very little work was being done now, only essential jobs such as cooking, water carrying, general camp maintenance and most important, treatment and care of the sick. We were given medical inspections and graded for travelling, the fittest men to go first. If your blood count was below sixty, you weren't fit to travel by plane. I was lucky and just made it. We had heard that a large number of men had already been flown out of Thailand to Rangoon, and we were all becoming restless, and anxious to be on the move.

But, despite all the evidence of the coming freedom, we were still prisoners. The Nips were still armed but we weren't, that is, except for our two British parachutists. It was certainly a strange situation.

We continued to eat all we could – we'd never seen so many bananas. Despite our previous diet, we were becoming sick of the fruit. Most of us rapidly put on weight. I put on a stone in a week. In the evenings we sat about with plenty of cigarettes to smoke, we didn't even have to wait for someone to go and fetch a light from the cookhouse. We now had our own matches to use. We drank native whisky or sacci, and on the whole men behaved themselves well. Some did get worse for wear and had to be carried to their beds, only natural I suppose, considering how long we'd been without alcohol, and the strength of this local brew. Too much of this type of sacci would render the fittest of men legless and unconscious in a few minutes.

There was a Victory concert with the Nips the subjects of the jokes, football matches, a sports day, and all the time we were becoming fitter and rapidly replacing lost weight.

All very well, but how the time dragged.

Then at last came the day, the 5 September 1945. The first party were detailed to leave the camp in the early hours of the following morning, en route for Bangkok. I was fortunate to find my name included in the party. This was certainly one to look forward to, not up into the jungle this time, it would soon be to Britain and home. Every man was fitted out with some sort of clothing, not all new, but at least we all had our nakedness covered, important – we would soon be seen by the civilian population.

There was very little sleep for anyone that night, the mood of excitement can hardly be imagined unless experienced. All that waiting, now this was it! Those not travelling with this first party were affected just as much as the others, after all, this was the real thing, it would soon be back to our homelands for all of us.

Before daylight next morning, we paraded, and after a number of routine checks, our party marched out of Tamuang camp for the last time. The wait on the railway siding was a long one, but what did it matter this time. Not a bit. We were on our way. There was plenty of food to eat, cigarettes to smoke and hundreds of things to discuss. The train eventually arrived, and for the last time we were crowded into railway trucks. There weren't any passenger carriages on our railway, but this time we would put up with any conditions, we were going home. We had our escort of armed Nips, but nobody bothered with them, they didn't shout or bully now, they were very subdued. No doubt they had plenty to occupy their minds.

Chapter 29

On the Move

> "What we call the beginning is often the end,
> and to make an end is to make a beginning.
> The end is where we start from."
>
> George Eliot
> 1819–1880

It was a cramped, long and tiresome journey, but our spirits were high and who cared? Passing through Non Pladuk station we saw hundreds of Nip troops in about the same condition we had been enduring two years before, after a year of captivity. They were in a terrible state, some appeared to lay dying beside the railway track. Badly as we had been treated, it was impossible not to feel sorry for them.

Arriving at Bangkok station late afternoon, we were supplied with biscuits, tea and more cigarettes, then ferried across the river to board awaiting lorries. This was the last we saw of the Nips.

We were driven in open trucks through Bangkok to the airfield, thousands of natives lining the roads to cheer us as we passed by. I think they must have thought we were Allied forces, we couldn't have looked much like them, but at this stage there were scarcely any Allied forces in the area.

At the airfield we had a good hot bath. Phew! This was different! How long was it since we had the last one?

A meal was laid on and we were split into groups of twenty five, and each group given the number of a plane party. It was expected that we would fly to Rangoon the following day, depending upon the number of planes available. We settled down for the night, but there seemed to be more mosquitoes in this place than there were in the jungle. It didn't matter, we wouldn't have slept much anyway. What are a few mosquitoes among free men?

Next morning, it was yet another bath and meal, after which we dumped all our POW belongings and rubbish. We were to travel only in the clothes essential to wear. Planes began to arrive, and one by one our parties were called into the hangar. On the way, we filed past a white woman and received tea, biscuits, vitamin tablets, metaquine tablets and more cigarettes. But, my God! A white woman! "French, wasn't she?"

There was an hour or so's wait in the hangar, during which time we were able to talk to the pilots and crews of the planes waiting to take off. It was all very relaxed and friendly, none of the old army "bull", to which we had been accustomed before becoming POW's. Our party number was called, we filed out of the hangar, and boarded the waiting Dakota.

It didn't look much of a plane, probably seen many days of continuous service without a great deal of attention being paid to its mechanical defects. As the engines turned, the whole thing shook as though at anytime it would fall to pieces. I must admit we felt more than a little apprehensive at the prospect of a few hours journey in this rattling machine. It didn't exactly appear to be held together with string, but not far from it. However, if the crew were prepared to fly the thing surely it would be churlish of us to object. We packed along the little metal benches by tiny windows, and within a couple of minutes were off. The RAF certainly didn't believe in wasting time. Glancing through a small window I could see the paddy fields of Thailand below us. It was goodbye to all the degradation and misery, we were on our way.

The flight could hardly be described as enjoyable, but at last we were free men, and this mattered above all else. We flew into turbulent weather and the Pilot climbed to over sixteen thousand feet to avoid it. The RAF medical orderly told us that pilots had been ordered to fly as low as possible because of our physical condition but the increase in altitude was unavoidable. We shivered despite the thick blankets he produced to keep us warm. It was noticeable that the crew in their shirt sleeves were completely unaffected by the conditions. Our blood had certainly become thin.

After more than three hours we landed on an airfield in Rangoon. It was pouring with rain but we didn't even get our feet wet. Stepping straight off the plane into waiting ambulances, we were whisked off to a Reception Centre where British nurses and WVS ladies sat us down at tables for a meal. A table and a chair! This seemed excess of luxury. For years we hadn't sat at a table, on a chair, or seen a meal like this. Knives and forks too, surely we hadn't forgotten how to use them? And these English girls, how long since we'd seen one, let alone heard one speak. Their voices seemed strangely high pitched to us. I remember sitting at the table, wondering just where to start attacking the meal, when a charming nurse put her arm round my shoulder, and asked me how I felt after the plane trip. I didn't know what to do. I just stared at her like a grateful animal with my mouth wide open. Was this heaven? I was certainly out of touch with things.

A wonderful meal over, our first real taste of civilisation, and the realisation that there must be even better things to come, we were once more in ambulances and on the move. This time we were driven in pouring rain to another centre for Returned Allied Prisoners of War and Internees, RAPWI for short. Here more sweet milky tea, and cigarettes awaited us. Particulars were taken and we received new army pay books, sent cables home and had preliminary medical inspections. Another short ride and we were in the particular hut, tent or building, which was to be our home for the next few days.

I found myself in one of the newly erected wooden huts, and allocated a bed to sleep in. Things were certainly getting better all the time. Here were clean blankets and sheets, something different to a bamboo platform and a single rice sack for covering. I went to a store and drew pyjamas, knife, fork, spoon, plate and several other items that I had been managing to do without for ages.

After another good meal, no rice on this menu, I returned to the hut, to find on my bed, more cigarettes, chocolate, a bottle of beer, airmail letter cards and a pencil. This just couldn't be real. I should wake up any minute in a rice sack!

About five days here, fitted out in green uniforms, at last reasonably dressed, we were allowed out of our immediate area. I made for the cinema. What a change in women's hair styles, was my reaction to the films. Lord Louis Mountbatten visited us, and I was impressed by his down to earth manner and language. He gave us snippets of information, answered a few questions and told us of arrangements being made to get us home. There was an opportunity to send more cards. Some chaps were lucky to receive some mail.

After this, there was yet another move. Together with four other men from the Cambridgeshires, I went to a unit of the South African Army Service Corps. We became guests of the Sergeant's Mess. Several more days pampering followed, but we were becoming very anxious to start the last part of our journey home. It would have been ungrateful not to have shown some appreciation of what was being done for us, but when would we leave Rangoon?

The eagerly awaited day came for the five of us on the 17 September, when we were moved to a transit camp and here issued with yet more clothing and kit. That night was spent in a tent. The rain bucketed down incessantly, but who cared, we wouldn't be working on the railway tomorrow. The following day, with several thousand others, we were taken to the docks in lorries, put onto landing craft and ferried out to the ships that would take us home.

The Allies seemed to be doing us proud. It was a Dutch boat this time, the MS Boissevain destined to be our home for the next four or five weeks.

We left Rangoon on the 19 September 1945, the voyage could only be described as being near perfect, as far as we were concerned. Good weather, calm seas and plenty of food, the like of which we hadn't seen or eaten for years. We were subjected to numerous medical inspections and were crammed full of all manner of pills and medicines. We had vitamin tablets "coming out of our ears". But it seemed to take a lifetime to get anywhere near the United Kingdom.

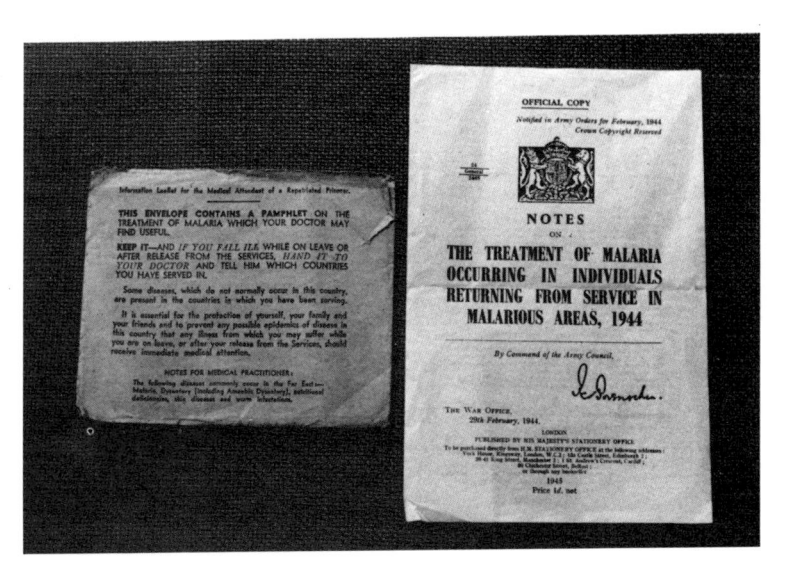

Pamphlet advising the treatment for Malaria.

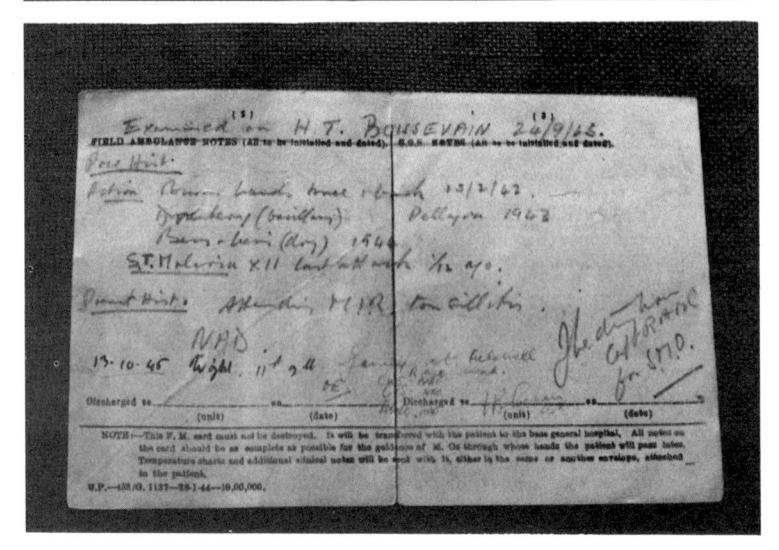

Medical card issued on board ship on voyage home. Could have included 13 bouts of Malaria with very little or no treatment, several attacks of Dysentery, Ulcers on legs and ankles, Scrotum Dermatitis, Beri Beri, Physical Exhaustion, Vitamin Deficiency, Ringworms, Dehydration, Pellagra, almost continuous Diarrhoea and possible injuries from beatings.

However, during those few weeks the health of most of us improved beyond the bounds of probability. We all put on weight and began to feel fit. It would have been difficult to recognise us as being the men toiling on the railway a few months back. At least our relations and friends would be spared seeing us in that condition; it was incredible what a difference the last few weeks had made.

And so, on the 14th October 1945, having left the good weather of the voyage behind, we arrived at Liverpool in thick fog and could see nothing of England's shores until our boat slowly nosed its way into the dock. On the quayside a thousand or more people were standing, cheering, arms waving as a band played us in. We had made it. There were so many of our friends that hadn't.

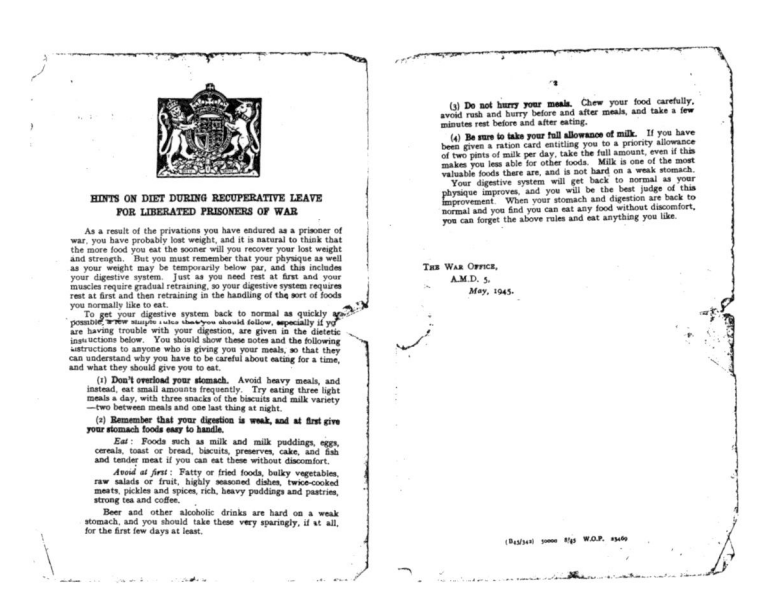

Hints on diet, how we should gradually allow our digestive systems to get accustomed to taking normal food again.

Chapter 30

Summing Up

"'No Report' (save hell is dark and we have just been there)"
G A Studdert-Kennedy

All this took place some forty years ago and I wrote at the time – "Somehow it was fitting to find England shrouded in fog on our return. What was everything like now, after the long time we'd been away? We felt as if we were returning from the grave to a place we hardly knew. What of our friends and families? Were they still alive? The majority of us were in ignorance. The fog typified our relationship with the old home country. Would the fog ever lift that hid the life of the prisoner of war in Japanese hands from the inhabitants of that right little, tight little island? Or would they be like the relatives of Lazarus and be unmoved though one came back from the dead?

Who in England can imagine what it was like to live in the Devil's Fun Fair that was Thailand if we ourselves find the memory fades? We shall forget; and forgetting is perhaps the best way out of the nightmare. Only occasionally shall I sweat with fear because I am looking into those distorted mirrors, where sound, strong young men appear swollen with beri beri, wasted with dysentery, twisted and mis-shapen by cruelty and pain. Maybe after the manner of the human mind I shall not look into all the mirrors, but make my choice, and only see the things I want to see.

What a good thing the mirror doesn't give back sounds and smells. Distortion of figure is enough without the reek of sickness and the stench of death. Enough to see the agony without hearing the cries of the tortured and delirious. In any case I can always close my eyes, when the hideous distortion of human bodies, makes my head damp with prickly sweat."

The fog did lift, as it always does eventually, and it would not be out of place to reflect on the fate or fortune of some of the characters I've mentioned, both prisoners and Japanese.

Bill Poel, the Dutchmen, with the bad leg ulcer at Tamarkan returned to Holland minus that leg. We traced each other and corresponded briefly. He wanted me to visit his family but unfortunately he died before anything could be arranged.

Bobbie, the female impersonator and medical orderly with me at Tamarkan was drowned at sea in September 1944, as was Snub the butcher about the same time. They were on board ships bound for Japan when torpedoed by the Americans. My other amputation case, from the Suffolk's, returned home and later managed his own Fish and Chip Shop.

The British Camp Commandant at Tamarkan, Colonel Toosey, returned to the United Kingdom and received the OBE for his conduct as Camp Commandant.

Snowy, the Sergeant, "have a go at anything" also made it. He returned home, lost a leg in a car accident but managed to run a business, as a builder, not a barber! He has since written and published a book.

Jack Darking, who supplied me with cigarettes during my spell in the "No Good House" also returned. I don't know what happened to "Ginger", the Sergeant Major responsible for putting me in there! But I bear him no grudge.

Lieutenant Kokuba, the Nip Camp Commandant at Chungkai, who threatened to remove my moustache with his sword, and I feared, with it my head, was sentenced to death in 1946. Not for this episode, I hasten to add, but the general ill treatment of prisoners. Colonel Ishi of Chungkai and Tamarkan and "Nobby" the horse doctor, received the same sentence but I'm not certain if they were carried out.

Colonel Yanagida also of Chungkai was sentenced to twenty years for ill treatment but subsequently pardoned. I've no idea how Taramoto fared!

Boon Pong, who I realised, must have been the big Thai with the smart white shirt and voluminous black trousers, his surname being in fact, Sirivejjabhandu, was awarded the George Medal for his services and the courage he displayed helping us during our spell as prisoners.

★ ★ ★

I suppose it would have been impossible to have survived these experiences without having ones life affected in some way. Like most of my friends, I learnt the value of many things and commodities normally taken for granted. Top of the list, without a doubt, must be water. How easy it is to turn on a tap and let this life saving liquid run to waste. Waste. Yes. Waste of any description is something I now abhor, particularly in respect of food. I also like to think that I gained some experience and understanding of human nature and as a result I am perhaps a little more tolerant to my fellowmen.

My life was radically changed in another way, a way which would not be readily linked to my life as a POW. I had been back in England a couple of years when on coming downstairs one morning, I smelt something that brought back vivid memories of Tamarkan. I traced the source of the unpleasant smell, a joint of meat purchased from the butchers the previous day, it had, as one might say, "gone off a bit". I looked at the meat. I saw it in an entirely different light. What I saw and smelt was a lump of rotting flesh on a limb in the ulcer ward at Tamarkan. After all what is meat, but flesh and tissue anyway? I took the odious substance into the garden and buried it! I became a vegetarian!

★ ★ ★

It was early, probably soon after six in the morning. What an unearthly hour they start raising patients in hospital. The voice of a young nurse said, in an unmistakeable accent. "Your injection, Mister 'Cofford'. It will not hurt." In the half light I saw the smiling face of a Japanese girl. It was 1983, I was in a London Hospital for Tropical Diseases for a routine check. For all I knew this young girl's father could have been one of my prison camp guards.

We both grinned. Not the slightest hint of any grudge or animosity here. She was no more to blame than I, for those three and a half years I had spent in Japanese prison camps.

Someone is always responsible for these bloody wars, but seldom the likes of her or me. I had no hate for this little girl or for any of her countrymen. Yes, there is much we should all forgive, and much for which we should be forgiven. But remember Bill Evans? And all those fine young men who died in the fighting in Singapore and later on the Railway?

Remember them?

Yes!

They must never be forgotten! Nor the thousands of innocent women and children destroyed or maimed by those two atom bombs!

Summing Up

Doug Skippen, President of the Ipswich Branch of FE POW's, finds the grave of a deceased colleague in the POW Cemetery of Kanchanaburi. This and the other photographs bearing his name were taken from a video recording made when he visited the area in 1987.

D. SKIPPEN 1987

Plaque at the entrance to Kanchanaburi War Cemetery. It commemorates those who died building the infamous railway.

Roll of Honour showing the names of some members of the Cambridgeshire and Suffolk Regiments. D. Skippen 1987

Summing Up 201

D. SKIPPEN 1987

The steel bridge at Tamarkan in 1987.

D. SKIPPEN 1987

Shows the type of diesel lorry which the Japanese adapted to run, and pull trucks on the railway.

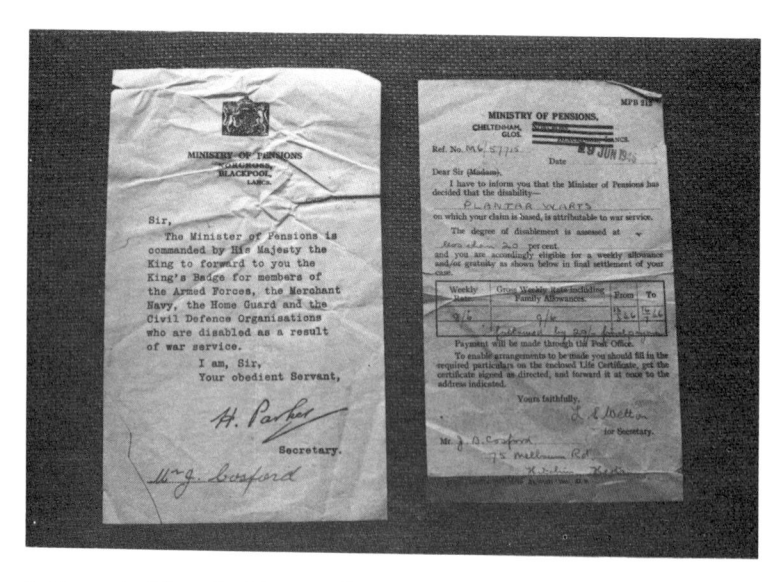

Letter received from the Ministry of Pensions when I was awarded a pension – the magnificent sum of 8/6 (42½p) per week for 13 weeks. It was for Plantar warts on the soles of my feet brought about through walking about in bare feet so long as a POW!

Photograph of me in 1987 after our home had been burgled for the fourth time, and the intruders decided to steal my war medals. Another story! Photograph by courtesy of Ipswich Mercury